THE LANTERN
AND THE
LOOKING-GLASS

THE LANTERN
AND THE
LOOKING-GLASS

Literature and Christian Belief

Nigel Forde

First published in Great Britain 1997
Society for Promoting Christian Knowledge
Holy Trinity Church
Marylebone Road
London NW1 4DU

British Library Cataloguing-in-Publication Data

A catalogue record of this book is available from
the British Library

ISBN 0-281-04906-8

Typeset by Pioneer Associates, Perthshire
Printed in Great Britain by
The Cromwell Press, Melksham, Wiltshire

for
Paul and Bernadette

Contents

Thy word is a lantern unto my feet: and a light unto my paths.

(Psalm 119.105)

. . . To hold, as 'twere, the mirror up to nature; to show virtue her own feature, scorn her own image, and the very age and body of the time his form and pressure.

(*Hamlet*, act 3, scene 2)

Preface

It seems to me that the *practice* of any art rather narrows the artist in regard to the *theory* of it, and I think I come more than most men under the condemnation, so that though I have read a good deal and have a good memory, my knowledge is limited.

So wrote the poet, prose-writer, designer and craftsman William Morris, declining the Chair of Poetry which had been offered to him by the University of Oxford in 1877.

And so write I at the beginning of this book. For I am no scholar. Scholars are men and women who have comprehended, embraced, absorbed the totality of their subject and all that bears on it. Scholars have facts at their fingertips, bifocal glasses and billowing gowns. I am a poet and playwright; poets and playwrights are more like Keats – convinced only of the holiness of the heart's affections.

So why am I writing this book? I am writing it because I rejoice in doing the work I do and in the work of other poets and writers, and I want to say why. I want to share my enjoyment with others who may have been denied, or have for some reason denied themselves, what C. S. Lewis called 'A wide and deep and genial experience of literature'.

I want to try to answer some of the difficult questions that scholars. on the whole, do not attempt because they take the answers for granted; and I want to offer a Christian critique – or the outline of one – to those who

have had that *genial experience* and want to explore it
further, but feel somehow that it must be marginal to their
Christian life or even that it might be immoral or dangerous: a primer in literature for Christian students of all ages.

There is, of course, no distinctive Christian *view* of
literature, any more than there is a distinctive Christian
view of suspension bridges, telephone systems or interior
decoration. But there are Christian principles involved
with all the matter that is dealt with by literature: human
behaviour, beliefs, morality, integrity, doubt, relationships,
ideals, and a hundred other things. These we shall look at
along with language and style, pattern and thought, symbol and metaphor, which are the means of literature.

I shall not, therefore, be saying, or even implying:

> You must read these books and no others. From them
> you must get such-and-such, and you must say about
> them precisely what I tell you to say and think about
> them just as I tell you to think, otherwise you are
> hopelessly lost and heretical and, not only that, you
> are vulgar.

We shall be examining how literature makes its meanings; what it can and cannot do; how we may judge it with
integrity even when it seems opposed to our beliefs and
(that fundamental question) why we should spend time
reading about people who never lived, involved in events
that never happened in places that never existed. How may
we, as Christians, respond to literature honestly, fully and
unblinkingly?

It has not been my intention deliberately to upset the
politically correct in my choice of words. It is for stylistic
reasons and for brevity that I have used the masculine
personal pronoun throughout this book rather than a combination of masculine and feminine. No bias is intended, as
the unprejudiced reader will soon see; it is just that I could
not countenance being responsible for a sentence such as:
'The poet combines his or her technique and his or her
imagination in such a way that his or her poem can explore

his or her . . .' etcetera etcetera. Nor, despite the example of Jane Austen, could I bring myself to write something that sounded as silly and clumsy as: 'The poet will not let their mind . . .'

Since this book is dealing with some of the most memorable and felicitous writing in one of the supplest and subtlest languages of the world, I have done my best to avoid the clumsy and the pedantic. So, except where a particular writer or critic is referred to, the masculine always embraces the feminine, as is customary in English prose.

When I said that this book was a primer in literature, I was not being falsely modest. Every point made might be expanded into a chapter; some could be developed into whole books.

What I have tried to do is set out some arguments and ideas that have not been much explored before, along with some that have been well-rehearsed, in order to give the reader a starting-point and a thesis which, like the navigator's sextant and compass, provide the means and the spur for further, deeper exploration.

Nigel Forde

Acknowledgements

—◦—

My thanks to the publishers who have granted permission for the use of the following material in this book:

Oxford University Press for lines from Christopher Fry *Venus Observed* act 2, scene 1, 1950; and Craig Raine 'On the Perpetuum Mobile' from *The Onion, Memory*, 1978.

Cambridge University Press for an extract from C. S. Lewis *An Experiment in Criticism*, 1961.

Faber and Faber Ltd for lines from Ted Hughes *A Choice of Shakespeare's Verse* and from Philip Larkin 'An Arundel Tomb' in *Collected Poems*, ed. Anthony Thwaite.

Macmillan General Books for the extracts from Barbara Tuchman *A Distant Mirror*.

HarperCollins Publishers Ltd for extracts from three books by C. S. Lewis: *The Screwtape Letters*, *Of This and Other Worlds* and *Mere Christianity*.

Murray Watts for extracts from 'The Angel of Light' in *Credo*.

I

*These be thy gods, O Israel!**

——◦——

Let us be absolutely clear about one thing at the very outset. The understanding, the appreciation, and even the creation of literature are not, in themselves, of supreme importance.

It is worth saying this for two reasons. First, because literature, even if we confine ourselves to literature written in English, is so attractive, so rich, so memorable, moving and consolatory; so enlarging to the imagination and the sympathies, so morally and ethically educative. It arouses the emotions and the intellect, the memory and the will; it wakes us up to the sublime beauty of the world at one moment and to its shameful corruption and decay at the next; it shows us what a responsible, tremendous and fearful thing it is to be a human; it reveals what is often hidden, and it teaches much that cannot easily be put into other words. Its concerns are those that we all feel when we can be bothered or can find time to feel at all: What is the truth of our existence? How do we know? Who are we? Why are we? What should we do, and why? It can make us laugh, weep, think, rethink and understand, as well as crystallizing for us thoughts and ideas which have drifted, half-grasped, at the edge of our consciousness. Literature is glorious. But its glory is not 'the glory as of the only begotten of the Father'. That belongs to another.

The second reason follows on from this. Writers have

* Exodus 32.4

I

been encouraged to give themselves airs. As if writing were
an activity transcending all others and its practitioners
worthy of awe and reverence. A published writer is deemed
to possess all sorts of attributes in addition to the ability to
craft an entertaining story. He is wise, prophetic, discerning; able to offer an opinion on marriage, the economy, the
freedom of the press, the ordination of women, euthanasia
and the function of the auxiliary verb in Cantonese. To hear
the words, 'Well, I'm a writer . . .' is very often to hear a
modern translation of:

> 'I am Sir Oracle,
> And when I ope my lips let no dog bark!'

Not that one should put the entire blame on the writers
themselves. Writing is a lonely and underpaid occupation
where success is not often in direct proportion to merit. It
is flattering to be asked to be a celebrity and be paid for it.
Few of us, however high-minded, would refuse to air our
opinions publicly. But while I would stay up very late in
order to hear A. S. Byatt, Alan Bennett or Seamus Heaney,
and always found it educative and provocative to listen to
Anthony Burgess, not all writers are as intelligent or com-
passionate, or use language as felicitously as they. To be a
writer is not to be one step down from God; even to be a
good writer is not, *ipso facto*, to have a hundred other talents conferred on you as if by a good fairy.

Now, unless you have been reading carefully, you may
think that I am setting out to denigrate literature. Far from
it. The rest of this book is going to be a passionate defence
of literature. But we have to be sure of our priorities. A
thing can be good; indeed, it can be very, very good – but
until we recognize that it can never be the highest, we are
not free fully to enjoy it, only to abuse it. We abuse it when
we give it the importance that should be reserved for God,
when we make it an idol. Now, literature may well be a
'better' idol than many others one could identify: alcohol,
sex, acquisitiveness, and so on; but it is still wrongly
understood and wrongly pursued so long as it remains in

the place that should be occupied by God. Whatever our senses and our proclivities may seem to tell us at the time, nothing can be enjoyed fully unless it is enjoyed properly, and to enjoy something properly means to understand and accept its relative importance within the whole scheme of things. This is well illustrated by a passage by a deeply Christian writer, Thomas Traherne:

> You never Enjoy the World aright, till the Sea it self floweth in your Veins, till you are Clothed with the Heavens, and Crowned with the Stars . . . Till you can Sing and Rejoice and Delight in GOD, as Misers do in Gold, and Kings in Scepters, you never Enjoy the World.

> (Traherne, *The First Century of Meditation*, 29)

Make literature your God and you lose God. Not only that, but you lose literature as well, because it will have been distorted, given an importance and a value that it was never meant to have and cannot sustain without even further distortion. Respected literary critics of the past such as F. R. Leavis and I. A. Richards made what amounted to a religion out of what was, after all, only an art form. Now they were not unintelligent men – far from it – and many of their judgements were interesting and valuable; but many of them were moral judgements delivered from a moral vacuum, since they saw literature itself as the embodiment of morality. Literature sorted out the sheep from the goats; the literature that one wrote or enjoyed determined one's moral status and one's fitness to be called human.

The problem with all this, as will easily be seen, is not that it is wrong, as such, but that it is a bit wrong-headed. It is not the whole truth. Literature deals with the ideas, the thoughts and the actions of men and women and is, therefore, a moral activity susceptible of moral judgements. But it is not *the* moral activity, and even implicitly to claim that it is makes for a falsification of life and, consequently, of literature itself.

Such a distorted view must always be expected if one

takes up a stance on politics, sexual politics, a particular school of psychology or philosophy and then tries to apply it, across the board, to everything else that one encounters. You end up with concepts as ridiculous as 'feminist gardening', 'Marxist car-maintenance' or 'post-Freudian candlemaking'. The trouble with such views is not that they do not have any validity at all, but that their supporters tend to claim for them an exclusive validity, and texts are thereby revered or scorned. Critics who ally themselves strongly with -isms tend to look no further than those -isms. Much use is made in their work of words such as 'merely', 'simply' and 'only', and these are not words lightly to be used of any occupation; certainly not one as complex as the creation of a novel or a poem. Whether or not we enjoy the game of cricket, it cannot fairly be summed up (and therefore dismissed) as hitting a bit of leather with a bit of wood.

Overstatement of any critical position leads to an untruthful analysis; it reduces the text to an illustration of the qualities the critic is looking for and tends to leave out everything else – especially anything that would weaken the critic's position. These qualities may be precisely those that other readers admire most. If we return for a moment to the image of cricket, we will find that the one given above is not, in itself, inaccurate, but it has less than a ten per cent accuracy: it leaves out the equally valid and interesting view of the wicketkeeper, the bowler and nine other fielders.

The Marxist critic, for instance, writes from the standpoint of a belief in the philosophical and political ideas of Karl Marx. It is arguable that Marx himself saw art as something of a special case, having an autonomy that might place it outside his central concern with the class-struggle, with history and with social history. This does not devalue Marxist criticism, even if it questions the wisdom of calling it Marxist. For such a critic, content is of greater importance than form or aesthetics. Literature is valuable for its evidence of social history and reality. It is certainly true that that is one interesting and valuable aspect of literature – of the novel particularly. If you want to understand the late nineteenth century, its slow process of industrialization and the effect on the countryside and its inhabitants; if you want to study the last vestiges of feudalism or the social structure of village life, then you could do a lot worse than to read Hardy. But to say, or even to imply, that such information is all that can be found in Hardy, or even that it is the most important thing, is patently untrue. It sounds reasonable in theory, but the first fifty pages of *The Mayor of Casterbridge* will be enough to convince all but the most biased reader that there is much more to him, and to any novel, than that. Some Marxists might even look at it the other way round and say that once you have studied the social history of the late nineteenth century, then you can judge Hardy as a novelist by how accurately and truthfully he recreates that period in his novels. Such an argument has as much truth as one is willing to allow. Even if it were demonstrable that Hardy's – and, indeed, George Eliot's – treatment of changing agricultural methods, commerce and the coming of the railway were factually inaccurate, it would not, for most people, invalidate the novels any more than Shakespeare's *Julius Caesar* is invalidated by the introduction of the famously anachronistic striking clock. That clock has been striking in more ways than Shakespeare envisaged; but it really doesn't matter.

What an author *must* do is remain true to the world that he has created. We would feel justifiably miffed if, in a comedy of manners set in Hampstead in the 1980s a character should disappear from her kitchen and, three seconds later, reappear in the Bodleian Library. If the same thing happened in a Terry Pratchett novel we would not turn a hair: he has created a world in which such things may happen. If a detective story writer can convince us that a man was murdered because he misquoted Keats, then we will accept that as sufficient motive, however dubious we may be about its likelihood in the world we meet when we close the book.

A Marxist critic, of course, would not have much to say about all this, because his mill needs a different kind of grist. Indeed, only a limited number of genres is open to Marxist criticism, which may be why some Marxists have added prescription (or even *pro*scription) to analysis – deciding on the sorts of art that should be produced. Composers such as Shostakovich and Prokofiev, as well as scores of Soviet writers, have discovered that it can be a very practical sort of criticism.

If the Marxist critic is almost exclusively concerned with the world 'outside', the objective reality which needs to be addressed, then the Freudian critic is at the opposite extreme. He is concerned with the inside; with finding connections between the author's biography and the worlds and characters that he invents. It is a speculative process at best, assuming, as it does, that we can understand an author and have sufficient information about his life and his mental processes. We need look no further than our most famous poet, Shakespeare, to see just how speculative the process is. More criticism – of every sort – has been written about him than about any other writer. But we should not forget that there is a good number of people who do not believe that Shakespeare wrote the plays attributed to him, and those who do have the minimum of biographical evidence to offer. Freudian criticism, like many other types, can certainly offer insights and truths; where it fails is in telling us anything genuinely revelatory about the poem or the novel *itself*. It is strong on the unprovable topics of motive, subconscious meaning and gratification of hidden desires, and very weak, as far as can be seen, on changing any reader's response to the text itself. So often it seems to imply that the writer is a kind of disease and the work he produces is discussable only as a symptom of that disease.

If, as the Freudians imply, we are all subconsciously Oedipal, or ineluctably motivated by sex even though we are not aware of it, why should that any longer be interesting or worthy of being turned into a critical criterion? It is as if someone were suddenly to realize that Henry James had two legs and to construct a critical theory around the fact. Soon it would be discovered that Henry Fielding had two legs, that Sir Walter Scott had two and that Jane Austen, if rumour could be believed, was similarly bipedal. If you study their works you will find that their main characters and several of the secondary ones are very fully described as far as colour of eyes, colour of hair, height and disposition are concerned. We know their qualities of mind, whether sympathetic, witty, clever, arrogant, shy, honest or surly; we are told of their habits, their occupations, their inmost thoughts and desires. But we are never told how many legs they have. Next case.

The main trouble with psychoanalytic criticism is that it is not susceptible to proof. Such a critic can have it all his own way. If one were to disagree with his findings, his answer is that you *would* say that, because you are, by definition, unconscious of the urges you are revealing and unwilling to admit to them. You can't win. And it would certainly not be sufficient to suggest that the critic himself was also writing from his subconscious and therefore displaying similar unadmitted urges to destroy or discredit. That would never do.

Freudian criticism becomes a useful tool when it considers a whole body of work, because then recurrences of images, symbols and ideas can be significant. It may be discovered that one poet writes a great deal about islands, another about uninhabited places, another about boxes, cupboards and containers of all sorts. We could expect fairly reliable conclusions to be drawn from such evidence about some aspects of the poet's psyche. But even then the interest will be, on the whole, biographical: it won't help in the appreciation of each individual poem as a successful or unsuccessful piece of writing. More is needed for that. Psychoanalytic methods of criticism are more prone than most to the thoughtless use of 'merely' and 'simply'.

Feminist criticism can, like all the previous methods, offer us fascinating truths and insights, whether it deals with new works or analyses literature of the past. It is probably more easily understood than Marxist or Leavisite methods, since feminism itself is much more of a live issue for every kind of reader, from the serious student of literature to the occasional reader on the commuter train. The truest way to understand such criticism is to go back to the eighteenth century and Mary Wollstonecraft's *A Vindication of the Rights of Woman*, which, along with Virginia Woolf's *A Room of One's Own*, provide the thesis for the present arguments of feminism.

I hope it will not seem too reductive to say that feminism questions the long-standing male ideologies and attitudes that have dominated not only the writing of literature but criticism as well. Men have had it all their own way, and where women have been represented, it has nearly always been via male prejudice and assumption. Feminist critics are asking whether there is an essential difference between the writing and thinking of men and women; whether there can be a distinctive feminine method or even language; or whether there is no fundamental difference, but rather an economic and psychological repression of women's writing and consequent undervaluing of what they have to say.

I hope it is clear by now that all these critical stances have something to recommend them; that their very particular methods have pointed us towards aspects of literature that we would be foolish to miss and blameworthy to ignore. If my tone has been somewhat grudging, it is because none of them in itself is sufficient. Why?

I think it is because each of them contains an implied 'ought'; each suggests that literature has some sort of 'duty', and that duty, of course, is to display and explore the concerns of whatever party is making the criticism. As readers, we will agree or disagree depending on the degree of sympathy we have with the party that is making the criticism. And, human nature being what it is, that means that what we agree with on Monday we may disagree with on Friday. It may be that this is a problem that cannot entirely be escaped, for, as rational beings, we must be open to argument and persuasion, we must retain the right to change our minds, to refine our opinions in the light of new evidence, new ideas and new revelations. But we need to start with a wider framework than a single issue, otherwise literary criticism will be reduced to a shouting of slogans. We must beware of bandwagons, however festively they are decorated; we must look beyond the moment, beyond subjectivity – though I shall have more to say about that later – and beyond our own private hobby-horses. As Dean Inge said, 'He who marries the Spirit of the Age will soon be a widower.'

An interesting book could be written – it may even have been written already – about plants in literature. It might explain to us the symbolic and mythical associations of shrubs such as bay and myrtle and how poets have used them. It might demonstrate how poets and novelists have made particular use of local flora in their work; it would notice how the tulip suddenly came to be used as an image in poems after its introduction to this country in the seventeenth century; we would hear about the holly and the ivy, the woodspurge and the daffodil. There would be a whole chapter on the rose. It is only a short, albeit ludicrous, step from this moderately useful and interesting book to a Horticulturalist School of criticism which pours scorn on any novel that ignored summer bedding or the potting-on of geraniums. Characters could be considered morally repugnant if they exposed their tender perennials to frost or failed to acknowledge the importance of double-digging. Stan Barstow's novels would be publicly burned as 'degrading to gardeners' or because they 'marginalized' the copper beech.

What, then, can we as Christians bring to literary criticism? Do we have a distinctive point of view? And, if we do, is it of any relevance? Indeed, what sort of relevance are we to look for? Relevance to our Christianity, or relevance to literature?

I think these questions have been partially answered

once we have rendered unto Caesar that which is Caesar's. Once we have realized that literature is but one pursuit among many; once we have admitted that though it may be a fine and praiseworthy thing to have written an exquisite lyric in a complex verse form, still that has nothing to do with purity of heart or Christlike behaviour; once we have allowed God to be God, and every other aspect of our life to settle into a subsidiary place, we shall be able to approach any art form with open eyes and minds; neither belittling it because it has failed to be a god, nor hysterically defending it because we need it to be a god.

We must forget, for a moment, what everybody else has required of literature, or perhaps even *found* in literature, and try to find out what it is and how it works. Only then can we judge its importance in the scheme of things.

Having put literature into a different box, as it were, from God, we must not expect it to stay there for ever. When Jesus said, 'Render unto Caesar that which is Caesar's,' he was not saying that our attitudes to money were not important, or St Paul would not have had to remind us that 'the love of money is the root of all evil'. If ever the flavours of literature are beginning to dull our palates to the flavour of God, then we must not be afraid to cut the offending literature out of our diet, however unsophisticated it may make us appear. There may well be certain sorts of literature produced in an age where reticence is not seen as a virtue which would blunt our sensibilities and lead us into temptation. It would be both an indulgence and a waste of time to list them, for we all have very different susceptibilities; but we should not be ashamed of avoiding such work, however trenchant, stark, fearless or frank the critics may find it.

But we should beware, too, of the opposite mistake: that of shutting our eyes and our minds to the realities of life. Even that great Puritan, John Milton could say:

> I cannot praise a fugitive and cloistered virtue, unexer-
> cised and unbreathed, that never sallies out and sees
> her adversary, but slinks out of the race, where that

immortal garland is to be run for, not without dust
and heat.

(Milton, *Areopagitica*)

We do a disservice to ourselves and to the world if we
underestimate the darkness that surrounds us and, instead,
seal ourselves into a sterile capsule of deliberate ignorance
and inaction which we dignify with the lie of Christian
'integrity' and whereby we hope against hope that the virus
of being human will never be able to infect our lives.

If we ignore or belittle sin, we ignore or belittle
redemption and the cost of redemption. When the theatre
company of which I am a member produced George
Peele's *The Love of King David for the Fair Bethsabe with
The Tragedy of Absolon* – the first extant biblical play in
English – this problem was encountered in a very practical
way. In that play, the excellence and the virtues of David
are very clearly shown, as they are in the Bible, as gifts from
God *despite* David's human failings. Evil is converted to
good, sin is transformed to righteousness; the child born of
adultery and murder grows into the great Solomon. If, in
an access of misplaced good taste, one skates over the
adultery of David, the violence of Absalom's rebellion or
the rape of Tamar, then the implication of the story is that
David's innate greatness or virtue has enabled him to rise
into his heroic stature. Not so. It would still be a fine story,
but it would miss out what both the Bible and Peele saw as
the most important point: that all the virtue in the play is
attributable to God. Repentance is David's part; redemption, transformation, renewal and empowering are God's.
Look, says the play, at what God can do even with such
rebellious and fallible material. If it is ever saying, 'Look
what man is capable of,' it is not in terms of heroism or
nobility, but of sin, corruption, fear and self-seeking.

Another script was offered to a Christian organization.
It was the story of Jesus, but Jesus never appeared; instead
we were shown the shock waves that rippled in his wake
among the people he dealt with. The script was rejected as
being 'too full of bad characters'. Comment would be

superfluous, but it would be interesting to know which version of the Bible these people had been reading.

John Henry Newman, in Discourse 8 of his *Scope and Nature of University Education*, wrote:

> If Literature is to be made a study of human nature, you cannot have a Christian Literature. It is a contradiction in terms to attempt a sinless Literature of sinful man.

One might go even further and say that the word Christian is meaningless except where it is attached to a human being. One can define a Christian. The problems begin when we come to talk of Christian music or Christian poetry. We have to decide, for instance, whether the word refers to the author or to the work. But to talk of Christian dressmaking, Christian gardening or Christian interior decoration is to talk nonsense, or at least potential nonsense. In what ways would a Christian herbaceous border differ from a pagan one? Can you really distinguish between a bread pudding made by a Christian and one baked in an atheist's oven? If these questions are thought to be too nice or too pedantic, then let me ask whether you would consider a picture entitled *The Transfiguration* or *Christ in the House of Simon* painted by an unbeliever to be a Christian picture. Contrariwise, as Tweedledum would say, if a Christian should paint a picture of Orpheus rescuing Eurydice from the Underworld, would that be a Christian painting or not?

There is, then, by definition, no Christian theory of literature; but neither is there any ready-made theory that Christians, by virtue of their beliefs, ought to adopt. The Bible has nothing to say about literature. We know where we stand on murder, covetousness, pride and sloth, but not on Shakespeare's sonnets or the novels of Julian Barnes.

And yet there is an implicit approval of literature to be found throughout the Bible, in that the Bible itself works through various literary genres. No better approval is needed. Of course there is history and philosophy and exhortation in the Bible, but between all these types of writing, and far outweighing them both in quantity and in memorability, we find stories and poems: Job and Esther, Daniel and Jeremiah, the Song of Solomon, the Psalms, Isaiah, Jonah, and all four gospels. Even when history is being recounted, it is done through vivid stories with dramatic shape, real characters, realistic dialogue, suspense and all the other techniques of the fiction writer. Genesis, Exodus, Judges, Samuel, Joshua and Kings swarm with some of the greatest characters and incidents that the Bible can boast. Perhaps the two least-read books are Leviticus and Numbers. It's not hard to see why that should be so.

Jesus, almost without exception, used literary devices in order to teach. Asked to explain something, he doesn't give an overtly spiritual answer: he doesn't talk about God, quote the scriptures or the commandments half so often as he simply tells a story. And what sort of story? A spiritual one? No. A modern, secular, unholy down-to-earth story, and often an ambiguous one. Often his hearers were rather baffled and annoyed. Could not their rabbi, their spiritual director, their master sent from God give them straight-forward, black and white, unmistakable instruction? Well, he didn't at any rate; he gave them a story without a moral. If they asked for a moral, or what we would call a message, he didn't tell them. 'He who has ears to hear, let him hear.' That is as much as to say, 'What do *you* think it means?' If we are called to be Christlike, that, I suggest, is a pattern for any of us involved in the writing of literature.

I have also been informed – and my knowledge of Aramaic is such that I must take on trust what I am told by those who have studied the matter – that the stories Jesus told, when heard in the original language, would have had a kind of pattern and rhythm not unlike that of poetry; they would, if that is true, have been even more memo-rable: vivid stories told in rhythm.

We must not, then, dismiss literature, whether it pur-ports to be sacred or is unashamedly secular. Some matters are, obviously, better dealt with in the form of a play or a poem or a novel than delivered as straight precepts. We know that by looking at the way God has chosen to communicate with us. God can be glorified in literature written by unbelievers, even if they did not mean him to be. Anything that wakes us up to the beauties and the horrors of the world, to the way we treat one another or fool ourselves; anything that wakes us up to the possibility of change, or healing, or the discovery of light through apparent darkness, is valuable and is ignored by Christians at their peril.

2

*The golden echo**

———∞———

A church of which I was a member once ran a series of lectures for its congregation, inviting professionals from various fields to say something about their own work and about the balance between what they did and what they believed. Many different disciplines were represented – stained glass, policing, medicine, music, architecture and literature.

After I had spoken on literature, a member of the audience pointed out that, while she had been very interested by what she had heard, she felt that it was a bit of a waste of time to read books which were not about the Bible or the Christian life; after she had spent all day at work, it seemed to her frivolous to occupy herself with a novel or a poem when she could be reading something useful – a non-fiction book written for Christians by Christians. Reading fiction, she said, made her feel guilty.

Now, I am not qualified to judge whether her feelings of guilt were well- or ill-founded. The *feeling* of guilt does not always mean that we are guilty, any more than a lack of guilty feelings points to innocence. So until we have worked out a satisfactory answer to the question, What does literature do? I am not going to beg it by saying that, of course, she was wrong. But I have come to the conclusion that her feelings, true or not, are far from unique

*G. M. Hopkins: 'The Leaden Echo and The Golden Echo'

among Christians, especially among evangelical Christians.

Since I have already admitted that literature is in a 'lower box' than God, I must content myself with trying to show how and why I think literature is important and enriching, and then leave to others the decision about whether they want their lives to be enriched in such a way. It is worth pointing out, though, that non-fiction written for Christians by Christians must also occupy a lower box than God. The question our audience member must answer is whether that box is lower than the one which contains imaginative literature. None of us can answer that question for her. Not that it is of extreme importance. Muesli may be a 'better' food than bacon, looked at from one point of view, and so may grapefruit; but is muesli better than grapefruit? And why not have both or all three?

It was interesting, too, that she talked of coming home after a day at work, but did not feel that it was pertinent to mention what she had spent her day doing. She was probably right; but what would we make of a person who decried literature for its lack of Christian values, its frequent conformity to corrupting influences in society, its removedness from the centre of true spirituality, and yet spent the day inventing meretricious ways to sell substandard products to people who might well not benefit from them, and if only in that sense, could not afford them? The words 'pot' and 'kettle' and 'black' spring to mind. It is quite possible for a Christian to hold very high standards when it comes to buying goods which have been produced by exploitation, dealing with companies that have a bad human rights record or that connive at environmental destruction, that advertise immorally, and so forth, but at the same time to work in an area which invites just as much suspicion.

When it comes to literature one is tempted to say, 'Let him who is without sin cast the first stone,' which is a fair challenge, though not an adequate defence. There is an adequate defence, which is that, unlike accountants, estate agents, insurance salesmen and Ministers of the Crown, the writer cannot hide his dubious morality or his false values: they are all there on the page for anyone to see.

But let us not waste any more time on this argument. It is patently obvious that anything, whether created by God or by man, can be misused, corrupted, made an occasion for sin; perhaps particularly – when the object itself is good – for sins of omission.

But what claims can we make for literature that might substantiate the conclusion of the previous chapter – that it deals with matters that Christians ignore at their peril? The Christian artist and poet David Jones has this to say:

> man is a creature whose end is extra-mundane and whose nature is to make things and that the things made are not only things of mundane requirement but are of necessity the signs of something other.
>
> (Jones, 'Epoch and Artist')

In other words, that literature is not a closed, self-regarding world even when it seems to be: it points to something other than itself. In many writers that 'something' is often the natural world; that is an important first step, because it shows that there is something other than ourselves that demands attention, and once we give that attention we find it turning more and more into a wondering, even reverent, attention.

It is perhaps the poet that points us towards nature while the novelist and playwright directs us to look closely at our fellow men and women. We do not and we cannot live purely as individuals; we were never meant to. We are a society. God himself is a society: the Father, the Son and the Holy Spirit, all three working as one. When God mused that 'It is not good that the man should be alone,' we can take that as more than a proposition about sexual relationships: it is just as true when it is taken to refer to mankind. We are members of a body which, by the workings of its various parts, is moving towards a unity and an understanding in all the areas that life offers to us: theology, of course, but science as well, and sociology, and art. We may offer our art to God, but we should realize that to do so will not render it *ipso facto* regenerate any more than art which is not offered will be entirely unregenerate.

Literature is all sorts of things, and we shall perhaps avoid a common mistake if we begin by accepting its ludic or playful quality; literature 'takes you out of yourself', it brings relaxation, entertainment and fun. It is a diversion. It is as well to notice this before we get on to discussing perhaps more serious aspects of literature, because even the most serious of texts must start here. If it does not grip and entertain or intrigue, then it is not going to fulfil any higher function with as much grace or depth as it might. Strategies have to be learned in order to get children to eat sprouts and broad beans; similar techniques must be employed by the writer if he wants to engage his reader with the discussion of important issues. The reader must be grabbed before he may be shaken or stirred.

Naturally enough, what grabbed readers in 1781 may find its power diminished in 1997, and readers of texts which are no longer contemporary may have to make a little more effort to engage with them. But once they do they will find that some kind of light is being shed on their own lives, fears, joys, desires and indeed character, even at a distance of several hundred years. Light travels very fast and human nature changes very slowly.

The most basic pleasure, then, to be obtained from liter-ature is that of diversion, refreshment. To escape for an hour or so into an imaginary world – even if it is very close to the one we know – can be an impetus as well as a delight. It can take us out of our own difficulties and worries and remind us that there is a larger landscape somewhere, a clearer air, a freer dimension than the one which is oppress-ing us at the moment.

This is not to advocate escap*ism*. Escape is something we all have to do from time to time; escape from routine, from solitude, from the throng, from danger. Or escape *into*: into the quiet countryside, the noisy party or into prayer. Escapism is rather different: it is to escape when what is required is to stand firm and face reality. Escapism is the habit of shutting one's eyes to the truth; the habit of never facing facts. The content of literature will not support escapism, though literature can, of course, be used in an escapist way.

Fairy-tales, for instance, are full of characters who succeed through endurance, humility, courage, fortitude; characters who do not shrink from the task or hide from the dangers. The one thing fairy-tales do not advocate is escapism. But if you are heedless of their content, you can send your days reading fairy-tales instead of starting the task, facing the creditor or whatever it is you are avoiding. That is escapism using fairy-tales. Don't blame the tales.

The next step up is the enjoyment of the cognitive aspects of literature. To put it in the most straightforward way possible, when you have read a book you know more than you did before you started. You understand something of what life was like on a frigate during the Napoleonic wars, or in the streets of Victorian London; in the trenches just before a bombardment or in the Highlands during the Clearances.

Now, it can be very reasonably argued that all these rewards of literature may just as easily be gained from reading history or journalism; and that, indeed, you will get a truer picture from either of these than you will from literature. This is no doubt true in a certain sense, but it is less true in another and, I think, more important sense. What, after all, is a 'true' picture of any event? Take these examples: 'The temperature is minus three degrees centigrade'; 'It is bitterly cold outside'; 'Tonight the wind gnaws/ with teeth of glass.'

Each of those sentences is giving, in essence, the same information; the first is an entirely objective, scientific statement which can be proved or disproved. If proved, anybody would accept it as unequivocally true. The second is a purely personal statement: its truth cannot be proved in the same way, for its validity depends on the trustworthiness of the speaker in the first place and on his experience in the second place. It is only a relative statement. A man used to the climate of South America would make such a statement long before an Arctic explorer would. What exactly *is* 'bitterly cold'? We don't know, but that does not stop us accepting it as a 'true' statement in many circumstances.

The last sentence – the opening of Laurie Lee's poem 'Christmas Landscape' – is entirely different in character. It is far from scientific; indeed, it is provably *false*, and yet it gives us a much more vivid experience of coldness than either of the other two statements. It creates an image that makes us feel and know.

None of these statements is the 'true' one. We cannot point to any of them and say, 'That is how cold it was *really*,' because reality is experienced on more than one level at a time, and the levels cannot be disentangled without the risk of falsificiation. C. S. Lewis puts it succinctly in *The Screwtape Letters* :

> You will notice that we have got them completely fogged about the meaning of the word 'real'. They tell each other, of some great spiritual experience, 'All that *really* happened was that you heard some music in a lighted building'; here 'Real' means the bare physical facts, separated from the other elements in the experience they actually had. On the other hand, they will also say 'It's all very well discussing that high dive as you sit here in an armchair, but wait till you get up there and see what it's *really* like': here 'real' is being used in the opposite sense to mean, not the physical facts (which they know already while discussing the matter in armchairs) but the emotional effect those facts will have on a human consciousness.
>
> (Lewis, *The Screwtape Letters*, no. XXX)

All of this calls into question whether history or journalism will, in fact, give us a 'truer' picture of the Napoleonic Wars than Forester gave us in his Hornblower novels and Bernard Cornwell in his Sharpe novels, or a more accurate picture of Victorian London than Dickens supplied in his massive output. In terms of what 'really' happened, the novelist supplies what the historian lacks, and vice versa. It is the historian's job to step back, to take everything into consideration, to give us a wide view in broad brushstrokes so that we understand what might be called the mechanics of the situation: the government decreed this, the armed forces responded thus, Napoleon failed to see that. We get one kind of knowledge from this approach. The novelist shows us the dizzying spin of an icy sea viewed from the top of a mainmast; he gives us the smell of gunpowder, the smash of cannonballs, the deaths of unique, individual men and women. That is another kind of knowledge; it is knowledge presented via the imagination, limited but immensely powerful and memorable.

The means and ends, then, of these two sorts of writing are different. But so is the intention. The poet and the novelist are not, for the most part, writing in order to rival the historian, nor to give an accurate version of history. What historical detail is available to their research they will not, of course, reject, but the detail and flavour that such research gives is secondary to their exploration of human behaviour. This is the third and most complex function of literature. We have already identified the function of entertainment and relaxation – story for the sake of a good story, if you like – and we have added to that something which is perhaps more of a by-product than a function as far as most writers are concerned: the cognitive aspect – learning the hierarchy of command on a ship, the sorts of carriage the Victorians travelled in, the weapons used in the Boer War, for instance. Now we have come to what may be seen as the most interesting and the richest area that literature deals with: men and women.

Should I have said 'Life'? I could have done, because that is what I mean. But I want to keep an important distinction here. 'Life' is an abstract noun, not a concrete one. Philosophers deal with 'Life'; literature deals with those who live it. From their experiences, actions, motives, desires, compromises, joys and sorrows, we build up a picture of what it is to be human. We find truths. Not 'The Truth', because literature can never discover that to us: it is in a different box; but lots of smaller truths which we can question and explore in order to give us some glimpse of what The Truth might entail. We will inch towards a solution to those questions about ourselves and the universe, the why, the how and the what that exercise us in our daily lives. Why we do it this way is summed up by John Keats:

> Axioms in philosophy are not axioms until they are proved upon our pulses.
>
> (Keats, letter to J. H. Reynolds, May 1818)

It is, in other words, the incarnational aspect of literature that makes it what it is. We may learn philosophical lessons but, as in the parables of Jesus, we learn them through the imagination. We learn because we have been a party to re-creation rather than to mere comment. We learn, if you like to put it that way, that 'the wind gnaws with teeth of glass' rather than that it is a few degrees below freezing.

We have already seen that what is real and true comes to us on several different levels simultaneously, and that none of them contains the whole truth and nothing but the truth, so while we cannot claim an absolute primacy for the imagination neither can we dismiss it as an important mode of understanding. Even as logical and apparently factual a discipline as mathematics can be grasped in its depth only by the imagination. If we are to believe the best practitioners, knowledge and logic will take you only so far, and then you need the help of the imagination. Hunches, intuitions and a sense of beauty all played their part in the great mathematical discoveries of the past, just as, one supposes, they will in the future. The imagination is *not* divorced from reality: it is one way, sometimes perhaps the only way, to grasp reality, to prove it on our pulses, and as Christians we should not fear that but welcome it.

Only thirty-five years ago C. S. Lewis could write:

Those of us who have been true readers all our life
seldom fully realise the enormous extension of our
being which we owe to authors ... The man who is
contented to be only himself, and therefore less a self,
is in prison. My own eyes are not enough for me, I
will see through those of others. Reality, even seen
through the eyes of many, is not enough. I will see
what others have invented ...

... in reading great literature I become a thousand
men and yet remain myself. Like the night sky in the
Greek poem, I see with a myriad eyes, but it is still I
who see. Here, as in worship, in love, in moral action,
and in knowing, I transcend myself; and am never
more myself than when I do.

(Lewis, *An Experiment in Criticism*, Epilogue)

Such an espousal of the humanizing influence of literature and its capacity for the completion and the healing of
human experience may find an echo in the minds of many
Christians today, but there is a growing reason to doubt it.
The trend today in religious thought and, indeed, in all the
most influential areas of communication, art, commerce,
education and the social sciences, is towards simple utility
or profitability – in terms of money, of course, not of
human growth. It is a trend away from the imponderable,
the intangible and the numinous; away from the intima-
tions of immortality. As Wordsworth asked in a poem
which takes that phrase as its title:

Whither is fled the visionary gleam?
Where is it now, the glory and the dream?

The modern imagination is a bit like the appendix: it is a
vestigial organ; nobody quite knows what it is there for,
and it is probably better to remove it so that it does not
grumble and interfere with the day to day business of
getting on with life. Man today must live by bread alone.
The imagination, whose watchword is 'taking pains', must
struggle to survive in a society whose watchword is 'labour-
saving'.

But the imagination is not an appendix. For the scientist, the artist and the theologian it is the one thing which might allow a glimpse of the Truth he is seeking for; it is the one thing that connects men and women to the universal. It transcends the here and now, it transcends but does not exclude the rational and allows us to experience lateral modes of thought; it allows us to feel, to wonder and to create.

That is what the imagination does. We are entitled to go further and ask what it is, but we must not expect a definitive answer. The mind and the brain, one would think, were easier to define, but half a dozen books about the mind have appeared in the last three or four years, all taking a different view, all quite strongly denying one another's conclusions.

The famous definition given by Coleridge has a great deal to recommend it. It places the source of the imagination squarely where the Christian would place it:

The primary Imagination I hold to be the living Power and prime Agent of all human Perception, and as a repetition in the finite mind of the eternal act of creation in the infinite I AM.

(Coleridge, *Biographia Literaria*, ch. 13)

People regard this as a difficult passage, but it seems to be quite unequivocal. What Coleridge is saying is that we cannot perceive anything except through the imagination. God is eternally creating, and that activity is echoed in our human, limited minds; we call it the imagination. So we may say that the artist at work – and this will be true of all artists whether they are confessed Christians or not – is emulating God's power of creation.

This is particularly interesting because it ties in perfectly with what Jesus said about his own work:

The Son can do nothing of himself, but what he seeth the Father do.

(John 5.19)

and that runs completely counter to the general late twentieth-century view of all art as 'self-expression'. To think of art as self-expression is the last-ditch stand of a feeble mind that is unwilling to take any serious thought and needs to find a way of justifying a similarly feeble-minded heap of rubbish produced in the name of art. It won't do; and it never did. How can one describe the paintings of Vermeer as self-expression? Or *Hamlet*? Or *Bleak House*? Or the poems of Pope? Even when we come to the lyric, personal voices of Wordsworth, for instance, or Hopkins, the word that best describes what they are doing is not 'expression' but 'exploration'. Self-expression can never be more interesting than the self being expressed, and our reaction tends to be: 'So what?' or a kind of embarrassment at being a voyeur. Even the most soul-searching poem does not do that to us. And, in fact, that expression 'soul-searching' takes us straight back to the idea of exploration rather than expression. Self-expression is externalizing an inward experience which is complete in itself, and it must be admitted that some unsuccessful literature does do this and does, as a result, embarrass us. When Tennyson or Shelley goes on automatic pilot or when Wordsworth allows his simplicity to degenerate into sentimentality, then the poems they produce are much more like self-expression than exploration. But literature cannot be judged by its least successful examples. When we talk of hedgehogs we do not include those that have encountered the school bus.

Take a poet sitting down to work on a poem. 'Why are you writing about that?' is a perfectly valid question to put to him. We are not asking what made him become a poet or why he has remained one: we assume he is one. Nor are we asking why he chose that subject; we assume it chosen. We are not asking what he is going to do with it when it is finished. There is no reason why he should know that. What we are asking is, 'What is the poem going to *do* for the subject?'

There seem to be two possibilities: either he is writing to

give people an aesthetic experience which he himself can get by simply looking at the object or considering the theme, or he is writing in order to explore his own experience of it; an experience which only begins to be realized as he writes. The poet writes not because he sees but in order to see properly. When we understand this we see that when writers say they are writing primarily for themselves this is just the opposite of a self-centred view. If you write to clarify your own vision, you are less likely to patronize your audience. Your art becomes not something you have and which you deign to scatter before others, it is more like a process where discoveries are made and shared. The self is active, but it is active among and interested in all those things which are precisely *not* the self.

The poet would probably add that, yes, of course you see something in the subject before you start to write about it, but only someone with experience of writing can realize how little that is compared with what you discover as your work progresses. If you write badly, of course, this does not happen, because your own scribbling comes between you and your subject and, after a while, all you can see is the vague waffle with which you have disguised the truth. But any good writer will tell you that he writes about things because, until he does, he doesn't know what they are like.

And where does all this discussion lead us when we come to consider the quality that contemporary critics seem to prize above all others – originality? In its purest sense originality is beyond us. We cannot create anything that is completely new, we can only recombine what already exists into new forms or find different ways of looking at the world. We may talk of discovering new things, but that is just an inaccurate use of language which makes us feel more original than we are. If we are discovering anything, we are discovering something old; we only call it new because we haven't noticed it before. The theory of relativity was considered new when it was brought before the world by Einstein, but if it is true it was presumably just as true in 1456, only nobody knew it. So while we may admit that we can discover something and that it will feel new, it will not be original.

If you had been able to suggest to a fifteenth-century poet that he should try to be original he would have looked at you in astonishment. Have things really come to that? The cult of the individual is a specifically twentieth-century one and, at its worst, is a recipe for conceited posturing where it is very easy to value a work not because it is in itself valid or true or important but because it is his or hers or mine.

Writers have, of course, been considered original and, if we are not being too strict about usage, the claim will stand up; but often it has been not because they were striving to be so but because they were striving to be authentic, to tell the truth. The originality of the 'metaphysical' poets came about not because they wanted to create a new fashion (though that happened as a by-product, as it so often does), but because they were trying to say much more difficult things – involving the intellect and the spirit – than the poets who were content to imitate the smoothness and clarity of their ancient Roman models. The very name 'novel' testifies to the appearance during the eighteenth century of an entirely new form of writing. And yet that was not entirely new either. There was Sidney's *Arcadia* in Britain and numerous Greek narratives by Chariton, Longus Heliodorus and others which have since become known as novels.

Even the poetry of Gerard Manley Hopkins, which struck his contemporaries with such force and bewildered his closest friends, was formed through a desire to be exact and specific and unmistakable, not to be original for the sake of it. Indeed, the rhythms and metres that he worked out were based on Anglo-Saxon verse forms from hundreds of years before.

It may be that if one strives for authenticity, if one tries to find one's own voice rather than ape the latest fashion, if one looks deeply and writes honestly, then originality cannot be avoided. That is when it is worth something.

T. S. Eliot wrote in 1955:

> It is a poet's business to be original, in all that is com-
> prehended by 'technique', only so far as is absolutely
> necessary for saying what he has to say.
>
> (Eliot, critical note on the
> *Collected Poems of Harold Monro*.)

That, surely, is good advice, implying as it does that originality is a last resort and not one to be sought for its own
sake. If we take seriously the words of Jesus in John 5.19
quoted above, we shall escape the worst trap that literature
sets for us: that of mere self-display and the assumption of
an authority which we are not entitled to claim.

For the Christian, any truth about this life should be
welcomed, but treated with suspicion when it leaps from
its box and asserts that it is the Truth about existence.
Literature is very good at seeing what is there and asking
pertinent questions about the way in which it affects us
and why it should do so. It is not so good when it is used
as a kind of substitute religion. We may rejoice in our imaginations, because they are the way in which we make sense
of all things, temporal or eternal, earthly or spiritual. We
must not substitute the imagination for God any more
than we would mistake the telephone for the friend who
rings us up.

The whole history of mankind proves to us that we need
stories; they seem to be built into the fabric of our
humanity. Apart from food and sleep, stories are the first
things that occupy us as children, whether we are making
them ourselves with dolls and cars and bricks and cowboy-
outfits, or whether we are having them read to us. The
appetite never goes away; it is fed in a score of different
ways from the saloon-bar joke to the fireside reading of
George Eliot, from Greek myths to detective fiction, from
Peanuts to *King Lear*.

We have seen that, although the Bible has nothing to say
about literature, it is itself a work of literature and uses all

its forms and devices. We have seen that Jesus himself used literary means in his teaching. Now we must try to find out what literature has to offer that is different from other sorts of writing; how literature works.

3

A man that looks on glasse[*]

Our minds are predisposed to find significance in whatever is put before them. We are used to seeing pattern, cycle, function all around us; and that is as true for the most atheistical scientist as it is for the Christian. Our minds force unity on the world of events and words and actions. We cannot imagine it otherwise and, indeed, if we could, it would *not* be otherwise since the very act of imagining is a patterning and significance-finding activity. Once again we see the likelihood of Coleridge's definition holding water: that the imagination is a repetition in our finite minds of God's eternal creative activity.

The mind is resolved on meaning, and it takes a lot to deflect it. Two proper nouns scribbled on a piece of paper: 'Monday. John,' holds no mystery for us even though there is no necessary logical sense that binds them together. From our own experience of scribblings on paper we can infer that someone called John was to be rung, met, written to or somehow dealt with on a Monday. We cannot tell any more without more knowledge. Which Monday and which John may still be mysteries, but the utterance or the message itself is not baffling.

There may, of course, be other explanations. The writer may have been practising to see if he or she could spell 'Monday' and 'John'. The word 'Monday' may be the last

---

[*] Herbert: 'The Elixir'

30

word in a letter of which the rest has disappeared, and 'John' may be a signature. If the writer were American, 'John' might refer to a piece of bathroom equipment, and there would be a consequent change of implication. It is certain that any detective fiction writer could find two or three other brilliant and, for a while at least, unguessable interpretations of those two simple words.

If that is true of a mere two words, how much more likely is it to be true of a whole sentence, a chapter, a complete novel. Certainly, as you add more words you do limit the possibilities of others, but you also pile up other complexities by bringing in such concepts as tone of voice, style and so forth. 'I must meet John on Monday' fixes more definitely the connection between the two nouns, but then we may ask whether that 'must' is said merely as a matter of fact, or is there an element of regret or anxiety in it? Is the word 'meet' significant? Is this something that has to be done face to face? And would Tuesday do? Would Sunday be even better?

Even when we turn to what is commonly called non-sense, the mind still strives after significance; and it is true to say that most 'nonsense verse' is very far from being non sense. 'Jabberwocky' even without Humpty Dumpty's gloss is an understandable narrative, as are all the 'Nonsense' poems of Edward Lear. The Yonghy-Bonghy-Bò may be a more unusual appellation than Malcolm but it isn't any more nonsensical; and to say that 'The Dong with the Luminous Nose', that great 'blues', that most heart-rendingly melancholy love poem, is nonsense, is itself utter nonsense.

Try to write sheer nonsense and you will find out how hard it is. I came up with:

> I sang a brass however stand
> And washed it into sides of hail.

Though it is difficult to work out what a 'however stand' might be, or how it could be washed into 'sides of hail', there is a syntactical logic about the lines which is far from

31

nonsense. A subject is followed by the right part of a verb which is followed by an object; after a conjunction we get a similarly properly constructed co-ordinate clause, and so on. It is not *utter* nonsense. Nor is it far away from a genuine poem. I meant it to be, but then I remembered this one by e. e. cummings, which certainly means and means very deeply:

> my father moved through dooms of love
> through sames of am through haves of give,
> singing each morning out of each night
> my father moved through depths of height

That is just the first of seventeen stanzas, but it is enough to show how the movement of the poem as syntax, as shaped, formal logic, makes sense of what seems to be an impossible statement. What are 'sames of am'? Asked that question out of the blue, one might be forgiven for thinking that the questioner was in need of a lie down; having read it in context, one might come up with something such as 'constancy of character'. It sort of means that, and it means much more, which is why cummings didn't use that phrase but wrote 'sames of am'. He is wrenching language around to try and make it echo that tremendous 'self' that he saw in his father. He has come up with something that is not only startling and resonant but something that is, like his father, unique. One could spend pages dissecting the poem, and this is not the place; but what gives the poem its power and transforms the impossible into the acceptable and even into the absolutely right is the way the phrase echoes the others – 'haves of give' and 'dooms of love' – the idea of his father not possessing anything but 'moving through', as if through a kind of eternal element that lay about him, and the subtle flow of the rhythms and the rhymes and half-rhymes. You begin to get a feeling of what poetry can convey if you compare it with a prosy reduction such as: 'My father was the centre of my world, constant in character, loving and generous.' The poem, by its very saying, says something quite different, and in a way which affects us quite differently.

A writer cannot escape meaning. I even, in a desperate attempt to write complete nonsense, resorted to simply taking the last words of a few poems and writing them down one after the other. Three poems by three different poets on a page from *The London Book of English Verse* opened (and you'll just have to take my word for this) entirely at random. This appeared:

> Die there, crest Death! Gate, dreams.
> How pure all.

Does not the mind even begin to see some kind of significance in that jumble of words yoked together by pure chance?

Whatever we read, then, we will take to be significant unless the matter is proved otherwise after a chapter or so. Where do we find that significance? There are lots of answers to that question. Let us get one out of the way to start with, since it cannot really be discussed in general terms even though it may well apply. I am talking about an accidental significance. A play or a poem or a novel that says something very particular to *me* in my particular situation at one particular time. Such things happen, and they are far from negligible; indeed they may in some respects be life-changing. But when you come to read the book again – in totally changed circumstances – you cannot find anything in it that could possibly move you so deeply and you wonder what on earth was so special about it in the first place.

It is still true, of course, that there must have been something *in* the work that affected somebody outside it, but that kind of effect cannot be foreseen or even, perhaps, wanted; so it was purely fortuitous, it was not an achievement of the writer and it was nothing to do with art.

The first significance of a piece of writing, whether poem, play or novel, will be its surface meaning; and that should be interesting in itself. When, in *Lord of the Flies*, William Golding's choir school survives a plane crash and finds itself marooned on a desert island with no adults, we know we are in for an interesting and unusual story. We can anticipate adventures, difficulties, unhappiness, delight, self-discovery and a great deal more. And we get it. But we also get something deeper. The subject of a novel, as our English teachers very usefully drummed into us at school, can be one thing: the *theme* of the novel is something different. There is a difference, as well as a connection, between the manifest content of a novel and the latent content, and the two are summed up very well in a famous stanza from George Herbert's poem 'The Elixer' (or, in more modern English, 'The Elixir'):

> A man that looks on glasse,
> On it may stay his eye;
> Or if he pleaseth, through it passe,
> And then the heav'n espie.

For Herbert, the whole world spoke of God in the same way that is suggested by St Paul in Romans 1.20. You can look at things, he is saying, and you can enjoy them without looking further. But everything speaks of something else beyond it as well as simply being what it is. The glass is glass, but it is also the means whereby you can see light. Herbert here is using 'heav'n' in both its senses: as the physical heaven, the sky with sun and moon and stars, which the window lets you see, and also as the heaven where God is to be found in his true glory.

One doesn't have to assume a Christian viewpoint in order to see that literature works in the same way. It is a 'glasse': you may stay your eyes on the story and enjoy it on that level, but you can also look through the story, for it is translucent, and see something deeper. Our minds search for significance.

In the case of *Lord of the Flies* it is fairly easy to read beyond the story of the small boys and to see the book as a kind of parable of human society. The 'world' run by schoolboys reveals to us aspects of the wider world run by adults. The story is a way of freeing us from religious, political and social affiliations, and all the prejudices they bring in their train, and showing us something of raw motive, the true springs of our behaviour – or what Golding proposes as such. The story is a way of questioning ideas such as power, authority and civilization without using those cold abstractions, but instead by seeing them in action.

Golding never tells us this, of course; and for that very reason we are freer to make our own response, judge by our own lights.

Again I repeat: the mind is resolved on meaning; it is the way we are made. What takes place is this. The writer tells a story. He says, in effect, 'This is what happened.' But, as we read, our minds cannot help but translate this into, 'This is what *happens.*' In other words, we take the story and translate it from individual significance into universal significance. We are able to take a tale about people who never existed doing and saying things they never could have done or said, and find in it genuine revelations about the way the world is and the way we work. We cannot help it any more than the writer can help writing something that resounds far beyond his avowed fiction.

Incidentally, we mustn't be tricked into thinking that because *Lord of the Flies* can be read in this way Golding has a thesis or an answer or a finished world-view to communicate. That would be to revert to the idea of writing as self-expression. What Golding is doing is exploring a possibility: 'What would happen if . . . ?' He writes in order to find out, and in order that we may find out. We are at liberty to agree or disagree with the possibilities he offers; and when we do, we find out more about what we think, how we behave and where we draw our mental lines.

Golding's *The Inheritors* and *Pincher Martin*, and to a certain extent his sea trilogy which began with *Rites of Passage*, could all be described, without doing too much violence to the language, as parables: they are stories which in their entirety can be taken on a different level. But while it is true that all literature deals with universal truths in terms of individual cases (this happened = this happens), not all literature is parable.

Parable nearly always involves the creation of a different, even an enclosed world. This has the effect of distancing us from everyday reality and even from our own morality, for such things do not necessarily apply in a made-up world. But then we are even more shocked when it slowly dawns on us that we are reading about ourselves. This castle of Franz Kafka's is the world we inhabit, or it looks enough like it for us to share his feelings of frustration and pur- poselessness. This landscape of Beckett's is one which we are often all too familiar with, and Vladimir and Estragon echo our own questions and fears. This crumbling ruin of Gormenghast created by Mervyn Peake is more familiar than we at first thought it would be; and wherever we travel with Gulliver we meet ourselves and our governors, our pettiness and our injustice.

If we have any problems with this kind of literature, they often stem from a deep-rooted feeling that art in general, not just books, should be an imitation of all that we see around us. Aristotle called this mimesis: imitation, reproduction. There is certainly a layer of that in most kinds of art. But it is seldom the main ingredient of any work of art, and it is mixed with a great deal of other material.

All that would be required of us when meeting pure mimesis is recognition. A man draws a mackerel that looks just like a mackerel and we say, 'Oh, yes, that is a mackerel.' End of man's relationship with work of art. But, of course, it isn't the end. Art is more than recognition, more than just a catalogue of our memories. Even a photograph is more than mimesis, if it is a true photograph. It speaks of the spirit of a person or a place by all sorts of subtle means – viewpoint, lighting, selectivity – and points beyond itself. If we simply want to jolt our memory, our slightly out of focus and badly composed holiday snaps will do far better than a genuine photograph. If we are after mere recognition, we shall consider Percy Edwards and Rory Bremner better artists than Shakespeare, Rembrandt and Bach.

But there are readers who will agree with all this and yet draw the line at true fantasy. Golding is acceptable because it *could* happen, and even *Waiting for Godot* is about two human beings, however oddly they behave. But what are we to say about literature, old and new, that deals with dwarves and dragons and Psammeads and phoenixes, with unicorns and trolls, with gods and with ghosts? The implicit objection is that they are unbelievable and therefore unworthy of serious literature.

I think that, in some ways, the reverse is the case. Mimesis alone is not enough; it lacks significance because it is concerned with objective reality, and what we want from literature is not just entertainment and play, not just the cognitive element – learning a few new facts about police procedure or the habits of the octopus – but to learn about human behaviour; to understand more about how we work as sentient, moral (or, indeed, immoral) beings. I think we can even go further and say that what we really need is to see humans in some sort of extreme. After all, every day we see humans chugging about their business, selling newspapers, shopping with three toddlers, standing miserably in queues, being cheerful at parties. We need more; we need to see our behaviour, our beliefs come to the crunch. We want to see people put to the test and, through the way they respond, we shall learn about or at least wonder about our own potential.

The form the test takes is not really that important, it just has to be appropriate for the particular aspect of humanity under consideration. *The Day of the Triffids* by John Wyndham will provide us with a good example. Its theme is that of man's courage, ingenuity and stamina in the face of a world disaster. It appeals to our basic instinct of self-preservation, of fencing ourselves off from all threats in a world that is ours and where we make the rules. Those at the centre of the novel surround themselves with all sorts of securities – food, guns, an electric fence – against the horror outside. It asks such questions as where is the dividing line between love and generosity and self-preservation; how human a person can be when all the appurtenances of his humanity, including society itself, have been taken away.

Now, in this novel the horror that threatens humanity is a triffid, a flesh-eating ambulatory plant that can stun from a distance and has previously managed to blind all but a very few of the earth's inhabitants. Is there really that much difference in function between a triffid and a dragon? They are both death-dealing, implacable and entirely other. Does it really matter that the arrow that can kill our hero is fired by an African head-hunter or a dwarf? It's the facing of the possibility of death that is at issue. Does it matter that it is a magic carpet or a Psammead that is responsible for Nesbit's children learning that the grass is not always greener on the other side of the fence and that actions have consequences, rather than that they should be persuaded into that belief by a lecturer in moral philosophy?

The best fantasy from *Piers Plowman* and Ariosto to *Five Children and It* and Terry Pratchett is concerned with inner reality, let the outer world be as it may. What we will not accept is impossible or improbable human behaviour, whether it is response to a dragon or a divorce, an Orc or an avalanche. These are devices that the writer uses to put his character under certain sorts of pressure and see how he reacts. Whatever the trappings of the story – even where the humans are, as it were, disguised as animals as in Swift, Lewis Carroll, Orwell and many others – we can judge the truth of the human behaviour that is shown us because we are human. It is the experience of being human that is being explored and tested within all these other experiences, likely or unlikely. Literature, as Lewis suggested in the passage quoted from *An Experiment in Criticism*, is a way of coming to understand and appreciate many different modes of thought, of behaviour, of awareness, some far removed from our own. Literature can short-circuit what would otherwise be a long process of learning from our own physical experience.

God has given us a world full of extraordinary natural things from amoebas to comets, from lichens to giraffes, from caddis flies to human beings, and the very least that a writer does for us – or, indeed, a scientist – is to say, 'Look! Listen!' He brings not only his own experience for us to examine, but the possible experience of hundreds of others who are fictional and yet behave in ways we recognize because it is human behaviour whatever the stimulus. Thus we understand more and we understand more deeply.

There are two worlds which we inhabit simultaneously – the outer world of things and other people, the world that contains us; and the inner world of our own hopes, fears, dreams, opinions and tastes, the world that is contained *by* us. Literature which works as parable is very good at dealing with the inner world, but that, of course, is not the whole story. There is a life of action as well as a life of thought

Thought and action are, to all intents and purposes, inseparable one from the other, and it would be impossible to have a piece of writing that was all thought and no action, just as it would be impossible to have one which was all action and no thought. They are interdependent, and a writer such an Bunyan, for instance, or Beckett, to choose a less obvious example, will use one as an image of the other. Bunyan imagines our inner temptations as people who talk to us and try to persuade us. Beckett, in *Waiting for Godot*, can use an old hat to symbolize the dignity of mankind.

We should perhaps visualize a diagram, a simple straight line. At one end of it, say the left, we place writings that are essentially thematic; that is to say, detailed realism, whether of life and landscape or of character, is absent or is at least unimportant. At the other end of the scale will come what we know as 'realistic' writing. By this I mean that the trappings of the outer world in all their detail and fullness are essential to what the author is doing. The work of Margaret Drabble would be a good example of that. In *The Radiant Way*, for instance, she is concerned to set down the ethos and the attitudes of the 1980s and of a Thatcherite Britain, and this involves a great deal of descriptive detail.

This is not to rule out any other significant themes which might be discovered in the book or to limit her to 'merely' cataloguing; nor, of course, is it to imply that the barer, thematic narratives at the left-hand end of the scale are less real; it is simply to give a rough and ready diagram to show us how different types of reality are formulated in different types of approach. Neither end of the scale excludes aspects of the other.

At the left-hand end of the scale we would put pure myth: the sort of story where plot in itself is significant – *Orpheus and Euridice*, *The Pardoner's Tale*, the fables of Aesop and La Fontaine, the *Mabinogion*. Here we would also place the parables of Jesus, *Animal Farm*, and most jokes.

At the right-hand end of the scale would come most of the novelists of the nineteenth century such as Trollope and Hardy, Stevenson and George Eliot. Right in the middle would come a writer such as Shakespeare, where the theme and its symbolic embodiment, where inner and outer reality, fuse and are inseparable.

One could play for hours with such a scheme, wondering quite where to place Jane Austen or Peacock, John Fowles or John Fuller; or working out how much of the left-hand quality resides in works that seem to belong at the right-hand end of the line. But there is something else that is interesting about this diagram, and that is that language itself is used differently at different ends of the line. The actual words used become vital at the right-hand end whereas, at the left-hand end, so long as the telling of the story is at least efficient, the words themselves are of secondary importance to what is being narrated.

This can be shown quite easily by reading a Greek myth

in two or three of the many different versions that are available to us. Robert Graves, in his two-volume work *The Greek Myths*, gives us a very matter-of-fact synopsis of each story, but includes all the details offered by dozens of different sources. The bareness does not matter; indeed, it seems to add to the weight of the significance that the story should be so unadorned. We seem to be in the presence of almost pure meaning, as is so often the case when reading the gospels. Ovid gives us very little more in the way of adornment, but the verse gives us more of a sense of immediacy and particularity which is further helped by direct speech, something Graves uses very sparingly. In Kingsley's version of the myths, *The Heroes*, a lot more flesh is put on the bare bones. The flesh itself is admirable, because Kingsley at his best has a command of prose rhythms and a sense of spaciousness that is a delight in itself. Try this passage from the story of Perseus:

> And he flitted on across the desert: over the rock ledges, and banks of shingle, and level wastes of sand, and shell-drifts bleaching in the sunshine, and the skeletons of great sea-monsters, and dead bones of ancient giants, strewn up and down upon the old sea floor.

There is nothing wrong with that as a piece of prose; the only question that arises, especially in the light of the other versions, is whether it is necessary. It adds another dimension, but does that dimension deserve to be there?

In an old *Children's Wonder Book* I have an abridged version of some of the stories from *The Heroes* and it omits precisely such passages without any detriment to the story. There are things, however beautifully they are uttered, that we do not need to know, that may actually interfere with the strength of the story. In the end it comes down to a matter of taste as regards which version we enjoy most, but we should be clear what it is we are enjoying. Is it the myth itself, or Kingsley's vision of it? Some love the pre-Raphaelite painters, but they should not claim that their pictures could ever be mistaken for something pre-Raphael. They actually shout rather loudly that they are *post*-Raphael. Kingsley thinks he is the 'glasse' through which we may see the Greek myths, but our focus is all too often *on* the glass rather than beyond it. So, although the myths belong at the left-hand end of our diagram, Kingsley has mingled them with something further along the line. Even when we have read *The Heroes*, though, what remains in our mind is the story itself, not the Victorian accretions it has acquired.

The point is this: in whatever words you tell the stories at the left-hand end of the line, you will not destroy them. The language in which they appear is not what is important about them. They transcend language. They exist by virtue of *what* they are, not of *how* they are. They remain at the root of all literature as a sort of underpinning pattern.

Tell the story of the good Samaritan in whatever way you will and it will have an effect. Change the man who is robbed and beaten to a woman: it doesn't matter. Change Jerusalem for Taunton and Jericho for Exeter: it doesn't matter. The power is in the story, not the words. The only danger is in adding too much. Stories at this end of the line are deliberately deficient in what we called earlier the cognitive element. You don't learn much as a by-product. We don't know anything about the man who journeyed from Jerusalem to Jericho. We don't know who he was, why he was going, his social status, his manner of dress, his world-view, his marital status, his bank balance, his age, hair-colour or whether he was even a nice man. When you read *Animal Farm* you won't find much detail about agricultural methods and practices; you'd do better to read Adrian Bell if that's what you want. And anyone who has ever told a joke knows that it can be told in a number of different ways, but what is essential is the unswerving trajectory towards the punch-line and the omission of all extraneous information and description.

Things are very different at the right-hand end of the scale. Here we encounter a very complex kind of poetry and the great realist writers such as Tolstoy, Hardy, Dickens and all their descendants – the modernists, the post-modernists, the surrealists, the magic-realists, and so on.

What we should notice first about this end of the scale is that, here, words are of the utmost importance. The medium is as important as the message. We have done with mere plot; now we have to deal with balance, and symbolism and character and motive. The novel is no longer so much about *what* happens as *who* happens, and nothing is unworthy of our notice. Everything is there for a purpose.

Have you ever noticed how, perhaps at work or in the pub, a colleague will begin to describe to you a book he has just finished or a film he saw that you have missed? He is terribly excited about it and starts unravelling the story for you along with some of the most impressive incidents or atmospheres. And you find it all hideously and ineffably dull. His eyes are sparkling and his knuckles are white, and all for this load of trivial nonsense which sounds as if it has been done a hundred times before. Sometimes – just sometimes – you catch a glimpse of what might have been an effective moment, a clever device, but it is soon carried away by the torrent.

You might, in fact, have been as impressed as he was if you had actually read the book or seen the film. For what has happened is that he has reduced something from the right-hand end of the diagram to something on the left-hand end and, in doing so, has left out what is truly significant and what, very often, impresses itself on our subconscious by a series of images or some other specifically literary device. You're not even getting half the story, and probably less than 5 per cent of the significance. It's not your friend's fault; he has tried to give you in ten minutes what the author may have struggled with for ten years, and he hasn't realized how much more than plot a novel must be.

The true meaning of a novel or a poem or a play lies in itself and in its entirety. It can never safely be reduced to what someone else has boiled out of it, or expanded to whatever someone else has read into it. Everything is there because the author put it there and has a reason for doing so.

You summarize for me the plot of Hardy's *The Wood-landers* and I will take away the impression of a lot of trees, a rather tangled love story, a bit of upper- versus lower-class warfare and a lot of silly misunderstandings. That is about as adequate a description of this powerful and most moving of stories as was our earlier description of cricket as 'hitting a bit of leather with a bit of wood'.

Where is that extraordinary episode of John South and the tree that grew outside his window? An episode that is a central symbol of how life and work and landscape are all tied up together; of how change can be longed for and yet still be deadly. Where is the episode of Suke Damson and Fitzpiers in the midsummer dusk? An incident which images one of the main themes of the novel and seems to assure us that our judgement of Fitzpiers is well-founded. Where is the tree-planting episode which relates so beautifully the troubles and joys of mankind to the whole of eternity?

> 'How they sigh directly we put 'em upright, though while they are lying down they don't sigh at all,' said Marty.
>
> 'Do they?' said Giles. 'I've never noticed it.'
>
> She erected one of the young pines into its hole, and held up her finger; the soft musical breathing instantly set in which was not to cease night or day till the grown trees should be felled – probably long after the two planters had been felled themselves.
>
> (Hardy, *The Woodlanders*, ch. 8)

At the right-hand end of our diagram, then, we are faced with a kind of writing that delivers a much more complex way of viewing human behaviour and values. It has introduced the idea of motive, which, as we have seen, was not a prerequisite of what we called mythical stories, and it has also introduced a demanding and uncontrollable world. Nature and man may come into conflict; society and man may be at loggerheads; love and duty, ambition and ability, sense and sensibility may all be at variance. In very broad terms, what has been introduced is an exploration of morality.

This, of course, was not entirely absent from the mythic, but it is worth pointing out that the moral, so called, of an Aesop fable is not so much an ethical point involving concepts such as 'should' and 'ought', as a picture of what life is like. Might is not always right, in a change of government the poor change nothing but the name of their master, no one truly forgets injuries in the presence of him who caused the injury, and so forth. One can even take a fable or a parable and use it to illustrate an entirely opposite meaning. Edwin Morgan does this quite brilliantly in his poem 'The Fifth Gospel'; and here is the third section of my own poem 'Demoralisations':

> On a high branch, shaded with leaves
> and green as a wave of the sea,
> hung a bunch of sour grapes.
> A fox with a long thirst and short legs
> tried for a whole sunstruck day
> to reach them, with snapping jaws
> and body flung again and again
> into the twisting wind. As he left
> the tree he reassured himself
> that the grapes were probably sour.
>
> Moral: You don't have to be
> successful to be right.

The parables of Jesus were moral, of course, but, in terms of the right-hand end of the line, they are unexplored. We take them as precepts, but we have to work them out in practice. What if the modern-day Samaritan had come across the battered traveller when he himself was rushing a child to hospital? This sounds simplistic – it is simplistic – but a novelist could treat even such a basic idea in an interesting and illuminating way.

The time has come to screw up our diagram and throw it away. It has served its purpose of demonstrating that there are different sorts of stories that need telling and reading in different ways; and what seems to be dumb in the face of our modern lives may actually have something very deep to say to us and that what seems to be a slice of life, will, by the very way in which its details are selected and its images recur and undergo transformation, illuminate our path like a lamp, or reveal to us our uninspected selves, like a looking-glass.

4

*Very like a whale**

———⌒◦⌒———

The process whereby every different sort of literature makes its meanings and shapes itself into significance in the mind of the reader is metaphorical. If, as we have suggested, a poem or a novel about specific events and people at a specific time is interpreted by our minds in a universal sense (this happened = this happens), then that piece of literature is working as a huge metaphor. 'This is just a story,' it is saying, 'but life is like this; the story is about you.' This is just as true whether it is applied to the mythic end of our now discarded diagram or to the realistic end. The whole of life cannot be dissected or explained, but, the author is saying, this will give you an image of the truth.

A whole novel is bound to be a very baggy kind of metaphor: there will not be one-to-one correspondences, there will not be characters or landscapes that 'stand for' anything that can be pinned down and examined, but that will not diminish the power of the metaphor. Indeed, it will increase it, in that other possible meanings and readings will not be closed off as they often are in a strict allegory. The truths that we discover in *The Woodlanders* are diminished if we consider Edred Fitzpiers as the spirit of modernism rather than as a weak, selfish and easily tempted man. Of course, there is something of the spirit of modernism about Fitzpiers, and we mustn't discard that completely in

* Shakespeare: *Hamlet* act 3, scene 2

47

our search for the true significance of *The Woodlanders*. He comes into a relatively unchanged community from the outside, bringing with him a whiff of science, a kind of glamour, and he occupies an ambiguous place in this feudal kind of society. But we must again beware of words such as 'only' and 'simply'; there is more to Fitzpiers than symbolism. Or perhaps we should say there is *less* to him than symbolism. As C. S. Lewis warns again and again, there is no story that the mind of a man can devise that cannot be turned into allegory by another man's mind. Unless the work is conceived as an allegory – and not much is, when we come down to it – it will only be diminished by forcing it into that mould.

Metaphor, however, is inescapable. Try to describe anything happening and you will almost certainly find yourself driven to metaphor if you want to give even the slightest flavour of experience or distinctiveness. Literal language is lifeless (there's a metaphor already) and is generally not even attempted except in legal documents. When birds wheel in the sky or the wind howls or the waves suck at the rocks, they do so metaphorically; when you browse through a book, drink in the view or plough through the snow, you do so at the expense of literal truth.

Metaphor is embedded (ah, there's another) in the language; it is part of our mode of perception, so much so that metaphors go unnoticed and, when people feel the need to be emphatic, lead to laughable constructions such as, 'It was literally bucketing down,' or 'The elm tree is being literally swept from our countryside.' Try to visualize that.

Those expressions – bucketing down, being swept away – are on their way to becoming what are known as dead metaphors: metaphors which are so much part of current expression, one might say cliché, that the figurative element in them is scarcely noticed. But it is there still, and the fact that we laugh when we add the adverb 'literally' proves it. One day they will join the truly dead metaphors. And what are they? Well, there are thousands; some are dead and buried in a single word such as 'arrive', which originally meant 'to come to the shore', or 'aggravate', meaning 'to increase in weight'; 'grade' no longer means 'step', and no one today notices the metaphor in the expression 'the bonnet of a car'.

The habit of metaphor is ingrained in the way we see and the way we describe what we see. In other words, we can understand things, see things, grasp things only when they are linked with what seems at first sight to be unconnected. That would be quite interesting if it were true only of our unstructured daily discourse and our simplest utterances. It becomes very interesting when we realize that it is also true of the densest, most highly wrought and significant linguistic device that we have produced – poetry. Language, at its least resourceful and at its most resourceful, is metaphorical: it tells one truth in terms of another, and in doing so points to a unity in the universe which we perhaps very seldom feel and yet which we demonstrate every time we use that one faculty which separates us from the rest of creation – language.

Is it not strange that this sensitive, delicate unique tool of language can only be used if it draws in and draws on the whole of experience and has to link itself again and again with the rest of creation? Is it not strange that man has invented the suspension bridge and Concorde, the particle accelerator and the safety match and a computer that can flash his own limitations back to him at immeasurable speed, but has never come up with any words that can explain to him what he means when he says 'love'?

Words are not inadequate to describe the steam engine; the forces and stresses acting on Spaghetti Junction and the Empire State Building have, by the evidence of our own eyes, been tabulated and communicated accurately; we have a vocabulary that can be used with pinpoint accuracy when we talk of shoes and ships and sealing-wax; but we can't describe the toothache or the sense of loss after a death except by drawing pictures in words, by making analogies. We reach out to the rest of creation to make sense of what we feel.

In other words, we are not allowed to be alone. The deepest part of us is also part of something else and cannot be understood without reference to all that surrounds us.

John Donne famously wrote in his *Devotions*:

> No man is an Island, entire of it self

which has probably been read, quite rightly, as meaning that man is a social animal who cannot exist on his own. This is borne out by the equally famous passage which follows:

> if a Clod be washed away by the Sea, Europe is the lesse . . . any man's death diminishes me, because I am involved in Mankinde.

But it is also true that 'no man is an Island' in his joys and in his suffering because language will not allow him to be; at these times when self seems supremely important and significant, he is being pointed away from himself, being forced to remove his gaze in order to understand. It is as if we were being told that the self is unique, is important, but must be seen in relation to a much bigger picture. It is humbling, but it is also salutary.

Now that we have seen that it is words which themselves point to an underlying unity of experience, reality and feelings, it is with a fresh vision that we come back to the metaphor that is so deeply connected with the person and the work of Jesus Christ; the idea of his being the Word:

> In the beginning was the Word, and the Word was with God, and the Word was God.
>
> (John 1.1)

The implication of this passage is that God and language are much more profoundly intertwined than we might have thought. To call Jesus 'the Word' is certainly a metaphor, but it is striking that it is *that* metaphor. Why, we may ask, should he not have been called 'the Seed'? or 'the Cord' that binds all things together?

For those who have a merely 'pretty' idea of symbolism, any image that has some sort of appropriateness and that does not involve a loss of dignity will do; and, quite often, when dealing with a facet of the nature or work of Jesus, they are right. Consider this anonymous poem which was beautifully set as a Christmas carol by Elizabeth Poston:

> The tree of life my soul hath seen,
> Laden with fruit, and always green:
> The trees of nature fruitless be
> Compared with Christ the apple tree.
>
> His beauty doth all things excel;
> By faith I know, but ne'er can tell
> The glory which I now can see
> In Jesus Christ the apple tree.
>
> For happiness I long have sought,
> And pleasure dearly I have bought:
> I missed of all; but now I see
> 'Tis found in Christ the apple tree.
>
> I'm weary with my former toil,
> Here I will sit and rest awhile;
> Under the shadow I will be
> Of Jesus Christ the apple tree.
>
> This fruit doth make my soul to thrive,
> It keeps my dying faith alive;
> Which makes my soul in haste to be
> With Jesus Christ the apple tree.

This has a mediaeval delight, rich natural and biblical associations and a painterly, almost iconographic devotional quality. But as a primary symbol it will not do. 'In the beginning was the apple tree, and the apple tree was with God . . .' sounds silly; and its silliness is not just a function of our long acquaintance with the opening of St John's Gospel, it is deeper than that. The image of the apple tree may move us but it will not shake us. We feel that Jesus may be seen as an apple tree, but he may be understood as the Word. The apple tree is not wrong, but the Word is right.

A symbol is, in the end, a profound and fearful thing; it is the closest we can get in metaphorical language to the literal truth, and that is why it affects us so deeply, beyond physical visualization, beyond etymology. The patina which comes from usage is not enough to explain the affective power of those two great symbols of bread and wine. Their power is inexplicable. No Yeats, no Blake, no Shakespeare could have furnished words of greater force or rightness. When symbols are true symbols we can never use the word 'mere' and we can never substitute anything else without falsification. Try it with bread and wine and you will produce something laughable and shallow. The key to symbolism is somewhere beyond the rational. You cannot find the source of a symbol's power. It is tempting to see bread and wine as somehow elemental, basic; but they are not. They are not as elemental as fruit and water, or meat and water. So the power is not in their God-given naturalness: they are both man-made. So is soup, and ratatouille and coffee – and even to mention those wholesome and nourishing foods is to enter into the realms of the laughable and the shallow when compared with those huge and resonant monosyllables 'bread' and 'wine'; just as the apple tree, in all its emblematic beauty, becomes merely fanciful when set against the idea of the Word, of Alpha and Omega, the letters which embrace all language.

Jesus Christ, then, is the Word. He is the means by which we measure and describe ourselves and everything that we experience. In him – as in language – reason, intuition, imagination and truth all meet. He is the difference between us and the rest of creation, for we share the nature of God in that we too may speak and not only, as in the case of the other creatures, be spoken.

But now comes another layer; the metaphor becomes something real:

And the Word was made flesh, and dwelt among us,

John tells us in verse 14 of chapter one. At last we know what we are dealing with and we can comprehend it, grasp it. But no, we can't; because that reality of the incarnated Word is itself a metaphor. The Word, if you like to put it that way, is still not the last word. One can almost hear patience stretched to its limits when Jesus answers Philip's plea at the last supper that he should show them the Father – God himself:

Jesus saith unto him, Have I been so long time with you, and yet hast thou not known me, Philip? he that hath seen me hath seen the Father.

(John 14. 9)

In other words Jesus is saying that he is, despite his tangible, real, humanity, a metaphor: the means by which we can begin to understand what God is like. God made us in his own image and then, so that we might understand, made himself in our image. Metaphor is heaped on metaphor.

We should not be surprised. If the objects and creatures in our own world cannot be amply described except by using metaphor; if our inner life cannot be approached except through metaphor, how else can we expect to grasp the 'otherness' of God?

When God is brought to the point of describing himself without metaphor, perhaps as the only being that can be described without metaphor, he is not, in terms of our human understanding, very helpful:

I AM THAT I AM,

he tells Moses (Exod. 3.14), and there is no more to be said. Uniqueness cannot be compared. Even Jesus, we come to understand, is not made like God: he has appeared to us in temporary and temporal disguise. His true likeness to God is in his qualities of sinlessness and perfection and sacrificial love.

Jesus never speaks of himself in explicit terms; his

person and his work is to be grasped through vision and imagination as, indeed, metaphor is always grasped. Even when questioned by Pilate he waits until Pilate suggests an answer before he will, obliquely, assent. And with the disciples themselves he is no less stringent: he waits until they know the truth. As Keats wrote:

Axioms in philosophy are not axioms until they are proved upon our pulses.

When Jesus knows that his truth has been proved upon their pulses, he will admit who he is. Not before that.

He saith unto them, But whom say ye that I am? And Simon Peter answered and said, Thou art the Christ, the Son of the living God. And Jesus answered and said unto him, Blessed art thou, Simon Bar-jona: for flesh and blood hath not revealed it unto thee, but my Father which is in heaven.

(Matt. 16. 15–17)

When Jesus speaks of himself he speaks in metaphor; he calls himself the good shepherd, the door, the way, the truth, the life, the vine, the light of the world. Unless we simply name him, we too speak of him in metaphors: the Son of God, the Lord, the King, the Prince of Peace, the Saviour. We pick out a facet of his nature or his work because the wholeness is inexpressible unless it is reduced to its barest terms – as in the words that came to Moses from the burning bush – which are so full that they seem empty:

I AM THAT I AM.

Such an expression is perhaps the root of the famously obscure or platitudinous expression of Gertrude Stein:

Rose is a rose is a rose is a rose is a rose.

The rose is its own explanation; comparing it with anything else diminishes it and reduces it to one thing among many, a sort of thing rather than a thing in itself. Which is true as far as it goes, and is certainly a healthy counterbalance to a view that would see everything as simply 'everything' and leave it unregarded as mere phenomena. But, if all that we have said about the Word and the unity of the world that it points to is true, then we must go further and, like Gerard Manley Hopkins, protest that this uniqueness is yet part of a unity which reaches its focus in the work of Christ; that, however individual each thing, each person may be, there is an underlying pattern and connection which both the musician and the theologian would call a 'ground'. Hopkins' most accessible exploration of this idea occurs in his sonnet 'As kingfishers catch fire', where:

> Each mortal thing does one thing and the same:
> Deals out that being indoors each one dwells;
> Selves – goes itself; *myself* it speaks and spells,
> Crying *What I do is me: for that I came.*

Everything, he is saying, is unique and bears witness to its own inner and distinctive self. Everything it does proclaims that individuality. So far we are still at one with Gertrude Stein; but then Hopkins asserts that the uniqueness he has identified is part of something much bigger and all-encompassing which actually, far from engulfing that uniqueness, is what confers it:

> Acts in God's eye what in God's eye he is –
> Christ – for Christ plays in ten thousand places . . . .

One can pursue an analogy until it becomes mere fancy, but is it not possible to see Christ as the Word – unique, individual – who creates other words, with a small 'w', all unique, all individual, but which are limited in meaning as is any noun, until they are combined into the pattern of the sentence, and then perhaps the paragraph, the chapter, the whole novel? Each word is itself and has its own meaning, but grows to a greater meaning when combined into a pattern, a language. We are not thereby prevented from seeing the rose as a rose or the kingfisher as a king-fisher; indeed, we can see more. A kingfisher in a glass case or even a cage is less of a kingfisher than the one we see darting and diving along the riverbank. Context is an important part of meaning.

Another useful exercise that our schoolteachers forced on us was to put a word into a sentence in order to prove that we understood its meaning. We were usually given pairs of words that looked similar but had very different meanings: judicious and judicial, uninterested and disinterested, enormity and enormousness. It was considered more fruitful to see the words in action, as it were, than merely to define them.

Humanity is 'proved' in the same way. We are unique; we have our own absolutely untouchable singularity which is valuable in itself and for itself; but it is not to be buried like the talent in the ground. It finds its true meaning in relationship, in interaction. I know that parts of me come to the surface only when I am alone and writing, but other no less valuable parts only appear when I am with my daughters. Particular parts of my mind and spirit are brought out by my friends in Somerset, others when I am rehearsing a play, others when I am talking to an audience. My 'self' is only a possibility, more or less realized ; a word that is striving to become a complete text.

Metaphor is the means whereby that text is composed; a reaching out to make sense, to find similarities in the seemingly disparate, to find a kind of order in the random. Before chaos theory became a recognized area of scientific study, literature embodied it, showing how a tiny flaw can lead to overwhelming tragedy, how the despised and apparently stupid third son of the miller can contrive success far beyond that of his pampered and cleverer brothers, how a momentary impulse can turn misery to joy, or joy to misery.

When we come to look at metaphor and how it works in poetry – the prime vehicle for densely metaphorical language – our theory explains what might otherwise have seemed baffling.

No one has ever been able to offer a watertight definition

of poetry, which is not in itself very surprising. Definitions are hard enough when they are concerned with the simplest things such as houses or tables; to define something as complex as poetry is going to be harder still. But all poets and all good critics seem to be agreed on one thing, namely that poetry gains in power as it deals with the concrete and the exact, and loses in power when it becomes vague and wafty and incorporates a great deal of abstraction. The poet must make us see, hear, touch, smell, taste.

We all know enough about death to reject a poem that simply says, 'Oooooh dear!' or, 'We all have to die.' Such a poem would be pointless and probably patronizing in that we are likely to have thought a great deal more deeply about the subject than the poet has. What we want from a poem about death is the particularity of the poet's experience which can fill out our own; images, perhaps, of the raw, brown earth in the green graveyard, the pain of seeing photographs, the tone of voice, the particular idiom that has gone and will never return. If we read about love, we don't want lots of hearts and souls and sighs, we want to know about Anthea or Lucasta and Julia, we want to know who and how they were. Bad poetry is constantly telling us 'how terrible' or 'how beautiful' or 'how funny', when what we need is a precise picture so that we can then imagine (not be told) how terrible or how beautiful it was. Dante Gabriel Rossetti is not my favourite poet, but his method of conveying grief in the poem 'The Woodspurge' is exactly right. The grief itself is off-stage, as it were, and we are never told – we don't need to be – what exactly the cause of his grief is; he knows that it is the tiny and apparently insignificant things that impinge on one's consciousness during moments of great sorrow or great joy; they become part of it. The nature of grief cannot be understood from these two stanzas (the second half of his poem), but we can recognize the truth that this is the way it affects us:

> My eyes, wide open, had the run
> Of some ten weeds to fix upon;

Among those few, out of the sun,
The woodspurge flowered, three cups in one.

From perfect grief there need not be
Wisdom or even memory;
One thing then learnt remains to me, –
The woodspurge has a cup of three.

And a contemporary poet, Craig Raine, describing the end of a relationship with all its awkwardness and misery, picks on a similar visual image that seems to be pure accident yet speaks emotional volumes without needing to describe the emotion:

In the cafeteria
we watched how drops on marble tabletops
are joined to trembling drops
by nervous fingers, how an upset teaspoon will
cry out with brief hysteria . . .

(Raine, 'On the Perpetuum Mobile')

The spilt water is his woodspurge; and he has neatly used words such as 'upset' and 'hysteria' but applied them, not to the two people involved, but to a teaspoon, keeping an emotional tension up but attaching it to the 'wrong' thing. We are almost forced to read the word 'upset' in a meta-phorical and therefore emotional sense before we realize that it is being used literally. But by then we have grasped both meanings quite clearly.

What at first sight seems baffling and which I think we can now answer is how a poem can exist on the very particular, concrete plane which is demanded of it if it is to be a poem at all, and yet have a vastness of meaning and inference that lifts it to the general and the universal – that makes it more than merely a poem about this incident, this object.

The answer is in the fact of the metaphor and the polar-ities of its meanings. In a metaphor we say that one thing *is* another, or, by the use of a verb we imply that we are seeing one thing in terms of another; making some sort of identification. A process which I have analysed as keeping individuality and particularity but allowing it to absorb other meanings as it is seen as part of a pattern or a process.

The truly successful metaphor – or simile – allows each part of the comparison to remain itself, at least enough for that vital part of it to impress the imagination, and the collision of the two in the verbal contrivance of the metaphor makes a third thing which is both more and less than the two things being compared and, at the same time, is different from both of them.

Reducing the process to a kind of algebra might help. When A is compared to B we get C, which is a new thing that is not just a combination of A and B but has a kind of energy and essence of its own. Enough of A and B are still present in C to make the comparison clear and exciting, but both will have been changed.

So it is fairly clear that metaphors have to be made carefully if the right amount of delight and verbal energy is to be produced. If the two components are qualitatively very close (a toad and a frog for example), the metaphor is likely to be inert and valueless. At the same time, if the two componenents are radically different, any comparison is liable to look forced and a bit specious (a toad and a Christmas tree, for example).

Thus, the interesting bit is the 'space' between the two things being compared. Such a space is non-existent in the dead metaphor: the two elements are conjoined in a muddy middle ground and can never be parted. We don't see the plough turning over the soil in a smooth bow-wave when we say 'the ship ploughed through the sea'; we don't see a little frilly hat when we talk of the 'bonnet' of a car.

But, in a real metaphor, the space between the components is where the reader's imagination can get to work, making connections via all five senses, via the memory of how such a such a word was used in *Twelfth Night*, or of how that phrase echoes another in Ecclesiastes, how this word, rhyming with that one, immediately sets up a connection which we are forced to notice. The distance between, let us say, a bee and a thought is unmeasurable. Make the two into a metaphor and the reader will leap into a rich imaginative space which is partly one which your verbal exactness has created for him – certainly one into which you steer him – and partly his own.

This is probably why T. S. Eliot spoke of a poem happening somewhere between the writer and the reader. The more exciting the poet's language and imagery is, the more the reader's imagination will set to. If the reader is lulled by vague words and woolly associations, his imagination will go to sleep and the poem will be moribund.

If we now add to the basic techniques of metaphor all the other devices that a poem can make use of – alliteration, assonance, allusion, rhyme, metre, word order, syntactical rule-breaking or bending, and so on – we can begin to see how it can transcend itself and begin to mean all sorts of things simultaneously; including things the poet thought he hadn't put there.

But even this is not quite the end of the matter. How many metaphors are there in a poem? How many images? When we come to inspect the structure of a poem, we find that there is the same sort of mental 'space' between different images and resonances and parallels as there is between the two components of each metaphor, and the interplay between metaphor and metaphor can be just as strong as the internal energy of each metaphor. In the end we find we have a huge complex web of associations and contrasts and parallels – all of which are going to be slightly different from reader to reader; sometimes very different without necessarily being untenable even if they were unforeseen.

Even the huge white frame that surrounds most poems once they are printed on a page has its part to play. It says, quite unmistakably, that this is not prose; that here we are going to find language used in a quite different and much more stringent way than we are used to in normal conversation, in journalism and even in a heightened use of language such as we would find in a novel or a play. A vast range of potentialities has been tapped; an almost infinite number of connections and associations can be made by an imagination put under pressure by language working at a much greater degree of intensity than we are used to. When language is in metaphorical mode it seems to be reaching back into the very springs of meaning; from words to *logos*; unlocking hidden truths, breathing new life, new vitality and new significance into what has become trite and tarnished. The time has come to remember Coleridge again:

> a repetition in the finite mind of the eternal act of creation in the infinite I AM.

And yet rational man longs for plain speaking. We want answers about the deepest things in life handed to us on a plate. Like the disciples when they heard the oblique stories and parables of Jesus, we don't want to have to work at the answers. We want to see the engineer's plans, not the architect's visions.

Even that extraordinary pastor and poet George Herbert felt a longing for more than images, verbal conceits, metaphors:

> Who sayes that fictions onely and false hair
> Become a verse? Is there in truth no beautie?
> Is all good structure in a winding stair?
> May no lines passe, except they do their dutie
> Not to a true, but painted chair?
>
> . . . .
>
> Must all be vail'd, while he that reades, divines,
> Catching the sense at two removes?
>
> (Herbert, 'Jordan')

But, of course, the paradox is that Herbert has had to resort to poetry in order to say how he wishes he did not have to resort to poetry. The best way to tell us truly that poetry is untruthful is by means of the poem's truth.

Just as God cannot say 'No' every time we put a foot wrong, if we are to be allowed choice and the exercise of free will, so neither can he say 'Yes' each time we catch something of the truth. We have to trust the light that is within us, seek for the truth and unity we cannot capture, watch how our words echo the deep grammar of the Word.

As Northrop Frye observes:

> The word 'spiritually' (*pneumatikos*) means a good many things in the New Testament, but one thing that it must always centrally mean is 'metaphorically'.
>
> (Frye, *The Great Code*, ch. 3)

If poetry is language under the greatest pressure, the most intense way of digging out the significance of what we see and what we feel, it is not surprising that it is to poetry we turn when our emotions are at their highest – whether it is the height of ecstasy or the height of sorrow. Even the dullest dog, finding himself on Westminster Bridge at four in the morning, might be heard to mutter to himself 'and all that mighty heart is lying still'; even the spottiest and most tongue-tied teenager might scribble a line or two of John Donne to his Rosalind in 3B.

Why speak at all? Because words, springing from the Word, are the proof of our identity and our value. We will make them ourselves if we can, but if we cannot then we will quote another poet because he will have found a way for us to catch, even temporarily, an inkling of our consequence.

Literature is a nation's memory as religion is its conscience. They are tied together inseparably and they remind us who we are when we are in danger of forgetting.

The poet lights a lantern which he hopes will illuminate his subject; and it does, but it also refracts, reflects, breaks up into different colours, shines into all sorts of darknesses, glitters on landscapes he has never imagined, and bends back on the reader as if from a looking-glass.

To look at one thing and understand it, we have to look beyond. Even to look inwards as deeply as we can, we have to look outwards. We are not allowed to sink and be lost in ourselves. If we want to find our true significance, we have to see ourselves as part of the ground and pattern of creation. This is what words teach us, and this is what the Word teaches us.

5

*The good and bad together**

Up to this point we have been considering the methods of literature and the way in which it makes its effects; we have seen how language and meaning are mutual influences but can be balanced in different ways, and we have seen how metaphor, the primary vehicle of imaginative truth, is constructed so as to be able to convey what at first sight seems impossible – a detailed, exact and concrete image that can have resonances far beyond the particular and speak of the timeless and the universal.

But the word 'literature' hardly ever appears in print naked and unadorned. It is nearly always to be found in the company of an adjective, and the two adjectives most widely used for this purpose are 'good' and 'serious'. The implication is that there is another sort of literature altogether which is neither good nor serious, and is probably not good because it is not serious.

Take the word 'serious' first. What is literature accused of being if it is not serious? What is the alternative to a serious literature? 'Unserious' will not do; that is lack of quality rather than a positive attribute. It may be philosophically correct, but it is practically useless to us.

All sorts of words are used – and, indeed, misused – as antonyms for 'serious': 'humorous', 'flippant', 'shallow' and 'playful', 'inconsequential'. There are plenty of others to be found in the thesaurus, but these five between them

* Shakespeare: *Antony and Cleopatra* act 2, scene 5

adequately cover the range of meanings.

We can get rid of one or two of them quite swiftly. If 'serious' is being used as an opposite of 'shallow', then it does seem to be saying something sensible. Shallowness is not a quality that has anything positive about it at all; it is a term that is always used pejoratively. It implies a lack of depth, intelligence and pertinence. Shallowness is never good.

'Flippant' we can also get rid of. Flippancy is a refusal to take anything seriously or even sensibly; to make light of what should not be made light of. It is the show-off's way of avoiding the issue. 'Serious' is well-applied to literature if it implies a lack of flippancy.

We are in slightly more treacherous waters when we come to the word 'inconsequential'. Can a piece of writing be serious and inconsequential? Argument about this could be long and inconclusive because, while flippancy and shallowness are qualities inherent in the writing, inconsequentiality is, more often than not, in the mind of the reader. It is a shrug of the shoulders and a 'So what?' What one reader finds inconsequential another may find deeply moving or challenging. Indeed, what may seem inconsequential to us at the age of twenty-five may become extremely important and significant when we are forty. I am probably not alone in finding nearly all Japanese *haiku* inconsequential to the point of pretentiousness, but then I do not speak Japanese, have a very inadequate understanding of Japanese culture and am all the more willing to admit that the fault is in me rather than in the poem since many people whose taste and intelligence I admire find them delightful and convincing.

Let us come a little closer to home. Perhaps it is something to do with my upbringing, my childhood, the fact that I am in Thomas Hardy's phrase 'a man who used to notice such things', but I find this (complete) poem by Edward Thomas packed with consequence out of all proportion to its length. To me it is of greater value than whole pages of Wordsworth:

Over the land freckled with snow half-thawed
The speculating rooks at their nests cawed
And saw from elm-tops, delicate as flower of grass,
What we below could not see, Winter pass.

(Thomas, 'Thaw')

But in some readers this arouses not a flicker to interest or enthusiasm. To me it is magical, not least on account of its plainness and its refusal of all poetic ornament. Mediocre poets cannot seem to resist the strangeness and spangle and glitter of snow; they wallow in it. But here there is not a word that we wouldn't use in everyday speech; not a twist of syntax; not an inversion or a conceit in sight, and not a hint of emotion. Hardly even a punctuation mark.

Here is something different again. Is it inconsequential?

The bluebells in your hand baffle you with their inscape, made to every sense: if you draw your fingers through them they are lodged and struggle/ with a shock of wet heads; the long stalks rub and click and flatten to a fan on one another like your fingers themselves would when you passed the palms hard across one another, making a brittle rub and jostle like the noise of a hurdle strained by leaning against; then there is the faint honey smell and in the mouth the sweet gum when you bite them. But this is easy, it is the eye they baffle. They give one a fancy of panpipes and of some wind instrument with stops – a trombone perhaps. The overhung necks – for growing they are little more than a staff with a simple crook but in water, where they stiffen, they take stronger turns, in the head like sheephooks, or, when more waved throughout, like the waves riding through a whip that is being smacked – what with these overhung necks and what with the crisped ruffled bells dropping mostly on one side and the gloss these have at their footstalks they have an air of the knights at chess. Then the knot or 'knoop' of buds some shut, some just gaping, which makes the pencil of the whole

spike, should be noticed: the inscape of the flower
most finely carried out in the siding of the axes, each
striking a greater and greater slant, is finished in these
clustered buds, which for the most part are not
straightened but rise to the end like a tongue and this
and their tapering and a little flattening they have
make them look like the heads of snakes.

(G. M. Hopkins, Journal, 9 May 1871)

It is tempting here to cheat and to say that the sensibility
that could see so clearly and find such a sensuous and
accurate way of setting down what it saw had immense
consequences on the poetry of Hopkins. There is a lot to
admire in this passage; even its unfinished quality, its lack
of punctuation and shapely syntax contributes to the sense
of excitement and discovery which is so much part of the
appeal. If it does nothing else, it does one thing that any art
must always do: it stops you and makes you look, forces
you to see. But it must be admitted that, in the wider sense,
it is inconsequential. It doesn't go anywhere, it is formless,
unstructured, even inaccurate if Hopkins thinks a trombone
has stops, but that dash may herald an afterthought rather
than an appositional phrase: Hopkins was very musical.
Writing may have great power and immediacy, as this
passage demonstrates, and yet be in the strictest sense of
the word inconsequential.

When, however, we come to the qualities of humour and
playfulness, only a fool would assert that they cannot co-
exist with seriousness. They are often the mode which
truly serious writing takes; there are levels of seriousness
that are best attainable and perhaps only attainable
through humour.

G. K. Chesterton was attacked by Joseph McCabe, a
man who, having left the priesthood, began to inveigh
against everything he had once believed. Chesterton, he
thought, should stop being funny and begin to be serious.
Chesterton's reply is a perfect response to that kind of
thinking:

Mr. McCabe thinks that I am not serious but only funny, because Mr. McCabe thinks that funny is the opposite of serious. Funny is the opposite of not funny, and of nothing else. The question of whether a man expresses himself in a grotesque or laughable phraseology, or in a stately and restrained phraseology, is not a question of motive or of moral state, it is a question of instinctive language and self-expression. Whether a man chooses to tell the truth in long sentences or short jokes is a problem analogous to whether he chooses to tell the truth in French or German. Whether a man preaches his gospel grotesquely or gravely is merely like the question of whether he preaches it in prose or verse. The question of whether Swift was funny in his irony is quite another sort of question to the question of whether Swift was serious in his pessimism ... The truth is, as I have said, that in this sense the two qualities of fun and seriousness have nothing to do with each other, they are no more comparable than black and triangular. Mr. Bernard Shaw is funny and sincere. Mr. George Robey is funny and not sincere. Mr. McCabe is sincere and not funny. The average Cabinet Minister is not sincere and not funny.

(Chesterton, 'Mr. McCabe and a Divine Frivolity', *Heretics*)

This is not only a perfect and reasonable answer, it is an illustration of the truth he is pursuing, being at once quite serious and quite funny. Humour is a marvellous vehicle for truth and seriousness, since what often prevents us from seeing the truth is a temperamentally fixed attitude, a prejudice. Armed with our stock responses, blinkers firmly attached, we are proof against mere argument; we have time to marshall our obstinacies. But humour bypasses the purely rational and takes us by surprise. Our defences are down before we have even seen the need to raise them. In the face of true wit or a real joke, we are suddenly enabled to see matters in a fresh light.

Scarcely any serious work – and I mean genuinely serious, not solemn or pompous – is completely devoid of comedy. Hardy's tragic stories are full of it, the novels of Dickens have it as their very element; Jane Austen revels in it, as do Pope, Johnson, Swift, Fielding, Smollett, Trollope, Browning, George Eliot, Mrs Gaskell and every novelist and playwright after, and including, James Joyce. There is no need even to mention Shakespeare.

It is certainly true that there are some individual poems which necessarily exclude comedy, but the poet himself will have many tones of voice. 'Do Not Go Gentle into that Good Night' was written by the same hand as *Under Milk Wood*, and *Childe Harold's Pilgrimage* comes from the same mind as *Don Juan*. Seriousness and comedy are part of the same vision. It is also interesting to note that if comedy will not be admitted intentionally, then the chances are that it will arrive unintentionally.

Life, after all, is at root a serious business, but even the most miserable of us cannot exclude entirely joy and delight and laughter. One of the prime sources of comedy is something that our very beliefs teach us; that there is a gap between what we should be and what we are. That divide between the ideal and the actual is an endless source of comedy, whether it be the dignified man slipping on the banana skin, the refusal of the shopkeeper to believe that the parrot is dead or an Ayckbourn couple striving for happiness in a world they cannot control. If literature is to be truthful, comedy must be as much part of it as it is part of life.

One of the interesting things about the best and most touching comedies is that they are always only a hair's breadth away from tragedy. When there is a real sense of dark and earthy danger in a production of *A Midsummer Night's Dream*, when one believes that these immortals, Oberon, Titania and Puck, could, if they wished, unleash utter and savage destruction on these foolish Greeks rather than mischief, however cold-hearted, the play takes on a new dimension and a new depth. *The Merchant of Venice* ends happily, but it has been a perilous journey and some nasty tastes are left in the mouth. What, one wonders, will marriage be like for Portia and Bassanio and for their two servants. The implication, for those who want to pick it up, is that it will not be all wine and roses; seldom, even, beer and skittles. There is a dark side to *Much Ado About Nothing* and a much, much darker side to *All's Well that Ends Well*. We feel that all these are comedies by accident; the material from which they are made would have served just as well for tragedy.

We might expect it to be just as true the other way round. One tiny difference and the tragedies would have become comedies. Had Othello taken the handkerchief as the worthless 'proof' it was, we might have had 'The Trouncing of Iago' or 'Carry On, Ancient'; had Macbeth gone a different way home, had Lear not wanted the best of both worlds, everyone would have lived happily ever after. There is some truth in that, but the likelihood is that we shouldn't have had a play at all, because the character driving it was missing. Take away Macbeth's fearful imagination or Lear's self-centredness and there is no catalyst; for while character is far from unimportant in comedy, it is not as crucial as it is in tragedy. Bassanio and Antonio don't bear too much inspection, but we will never get to the bottom of Hamlet's character. Plot is enough to set a comedy going and characters can be developed and discovered on the way. Tragedy needs a massive character with a dreadful flaw to precipitate the action, otherwise it is not a tragedy at all but just a nasty mess or a rather horrid accident.

Perhaps we should be content to say that comedy and tragedy are inseparable in our lives and in our literature, they are constant and inevitable conditions of what it means to be alive and to be human. To say, therefore, that one is 'serious' and one is not is to make a very fundamental error. If 'serious' means anything at all, it means more than 'straight-faced'.

The resurrection is a good example. Are we to say that

because the resurrection was the biggest surprise in history, the greatest cause for delight and joy and laughter and optimism, it was not serious? It is far, far more serious than the crucifixion.

It is surely more than accident that the funniest incident in the Bible is placed by Luke within a few verses of the crucifixion and burial of Jesus: the passage known as The Road to Emmaus. Two disciples are walking the seven or so miles from Jerusalem to Emmaus, weary and miserable. They are joined by Jesus but neither of them recognizes him and they begin to pour out their sorrows. Jesus doesn't let on, but nods and sympathizes and draws them out to tell him the whole story. Then, as they trudge on, he gives them a massive Bible study on the inevitability of Christ's death. We know who Jesus is, and this passage is the archetype of the famous 'cross-purposes' sketch that has provided staple comedy for Hancock or *Dad's Army*, Morecambe and Wise, The Two Ronnies and every sitcom that was ever written. But that's not the end of it.

When the disciples arrive home, they invite Jesus for supper. Suddenly, as he breaks the bread, some character-istic gesture gives him away and their eyes are opened. But at that moment he vanishes. Then, footsore and exhausted though they must be, they run all the way back down the road they have just travelled and into Jerusalem to break the good news. Only to be greeted with 'Yes, we know: he has just been here . . .'

If we go right back to Genesis and the story of Abraham and Sarah, we will discover that God's promised leadership of his chosen people begins with their son, Isaac. 'Isaac' is Hebrew for 'laughter'. God's own covenant is founded on laughter.

There remains one word to look at; a word which is used by many when they wish to imply a lack of seriousness in literature – playful.

We have already touched on this quality in chapters 2 and 3 where we discovered it to be an essential element of literature in the sense that it starts out by admitting that it is not true in a factual, historical way; that we start with a 'What if ... ?' or a 'Just suppose ...'. Literature must, in that sense, be ludic or it is not literature. But that would be admitted by the severest of critics. What is more often meant by 'playful' is a lightness of touch which, it is implied, goes ill with a seriousness of intent, or a wasting of time and energy on matters that have no pertinence in our life and destiny.

So let us look at what the word actually means, and let us look at those in our community whom we know to be the most playful of all, and see if anything can be learned.

'Play' comes from the Anglo-Saxon word 'plega', which certainly means what we would describe as play – a game, a sport; but it also means a fight or a battle. So if, as we are fond of repeating, drama is conflict, it should be no surprise that what we see in a theatre is called a play. We might be surprised, though, to realize that we can properly describe two men punching each other in the street as 'playing'.

We have used the word 'play' in that sense before, though we may not have noticed it, when we talk of 'the play of different forces' on a boat's hull, or 'the play of light and shade through the leaves' that falls on the grass, and in the emotions 'that played across his face'. And did we think of 'play' only in the gamesome sense? We probably did, for the idea of play as battle or struggle is, if not a dead metaphor, a moribund one. But in the phrases just quoted we can see that the sense is really of struggle and conflict, not of play in a sportive sense at all. The light and shade are struggling for supremacy, not having fun; the forces are in conflict, and so are the emotions. We have not lost that sense, even though we have hidden it from ourselves. The same is true of the word 'playful': it is, far from a criticism, a perfect description of literature.

And who are the most playful members of our community? Interestingly, whether we take playful to mean sportive and fun-making, or prone to conflict and the ups and down of life, the answer is children.

I will leave aside now the idea of conflict and battle as

part of our definition of play: when we talk about children playing, what is certainly uppermost in our minds is the fun and the make-believe. But if our critic was only referring to this when he implied that playfulness was not serious, he would still be wrong.

Play is a learning process. Providence has been kind in ensuring that education and having fun are synonymous, at least until adults get hold of the process. The most old-fashioned of parents and the most modern of child-psychologists seem remarkably to agree on the fact that play is good for children. When they are out climbing and running and jumping streams and kicking footballs, they are putting on physical muscle which their adult bodies need; when they are building and drawing, when they are being pirates, knights, smugglers, detectives, cowboys and indians, spacemen or supermen, they are, through experiment and role-play, putting on mental muscle. When they sit and think and wonder – and perhaps some of us can remember that this was no small part of childhood – they are putting on both mental and spiritual muscle. Feeding the imagination is as essential to health as feeding the body. The best literature, the most imaginative and enriching, will be playful and, in being so, will attain to the highest seriousness.

The best books for children are excellent books for adults. To paraphrase Dr Johnson, the man who is tired of Joan Aiken, E. Nesbit, Richmal Crompton, Alan Garner, Beatrix Potter, old Andersen, Uttley and Storr, is tired of life; and, indeed, exhausted of wonder. The difference between books 'for children' by these authors – and many others that could be mentioned – and books 'for adults' is minimal. It is not to be found in the matter of truth to experience, in the themes tackled, the relationships, or the subtlety of ideas and characterization. Joan Aiken's Mortimer the raven and Nesbit's Oswald Bastable are characters as great and as timeless as those created by Shakespeare and Dickens. Nor is it always to be found in a lack of linguistic sophistication. The main difference seems to be that the principal characters in books for children are children, and I cannot see why that should be a reason for dismay. To see one's adulthood as being in some way threatened or compromised by enjoying a story about children is a fair pointer to the fact that one is not yet really an adult.

Questions of taste can, of course, be involved; but one should realize that they are, truly, matters of taste and, as such, neither here nor there. If I enjoy courgettes but not celery, grapefruit but not bananas, and you enjoy just the opposite, we must agree to differ; for, although tastes can be acquired, it is doubtful whether argument or persuasion will play much of a part in the process.

What we must not do is fulminate against each other and call each other's tastes bad simply because we do not share them. I can understand, though I do not share, an aversion to animals dressed up – literally or metaphorically or both – as humans. Anyone with such an aversion will not find pleasure in Beatrix Potter, or *Animal Farm* or *The Wind in the Willows* or William Horwood's *Duncton Chronicles* or Adams' *Watership Down*. It will be no use to plead that *The Wind in the Willows* is one of the most successful literary embodiments of what we mean by the idea of 'home' or 'belonging', or that the *Duncton Chronicles* is an exploration of religious bigotry and truth. Celery and bananas may be full of vitamins and other invisible nourishment, but I'll get them from somewhere else, thank you very much.

Having examined the word 'serious' as a fitting adjective for literature, we have slipped, almost without noticing it, into inspecting what we mean when we talk about 'good' literature.

Because we are social beings, our taste in various matters is very much bound up with our self-image, our desire to be, or at least appear to be, intelligent, informed, right-thinking – all that can be subsumed by the word 'acceptable'. Since this is so, it might be as well to look at how we use the word 'good' in other contexts before we turn to such shaky and emotive ground.

What is a good car? There are dozens of possible answers. For one person it might be any old thing that has a low petrol consumption and high reliability. For another it might be one that emitted the fewest pollutants; for another it would be the nearest thing he could get to his own sitting-room, with superb stereo, air-conditioning, real wood and leather, and so forth; again, it might be one that went from nought to sixty in four and a half seconds or one that was strong on safety, or one that attracted attention outside the pub on a Saturday morning. In the same way, a good meal would be defined very differently by a dietician, a glutton, a schoolboy and a Frenchman. In other words, it all depends what you're looking for.

On the other hand, there is some overlap. Nobody would really consider a car to be good if it broke down every ten miles or could not be used in rain and snow. Even a dietician would agree that salads can be limp and boring affairs while a burger and chips may be exquisitely cooked. Examples could be multiplied, but what we seem to be discovering is that there is in each thing an inherent quality which, when it is realized, we call good. This does not mean to say that we have to like it. We may agree that a good lawn is one of thickly growing green grass, soft springy, comfortable to walk on and, in its smooth, mono-chrome sweep, setting off the mosaic of colours and shapes in the flower beds and borders; one with no weeds and no bare, brown patches. But we may prefer our daisy- and dandelion-strewn lawn; we may love the mosses that grow in its danker corners and the pheasants that peck it to ribbons.

All this is obvious enough, but it leads us to a conclusion that is the very opposite of the one that we so often adopt without noticing it: 'good' does not mean 'I like' and 'bad' does not mean 'I dislike'. We need a better criterion for good literature than that it should be to our personal taste.

The trouble is that, as in the case of the car, good is not an easily definable term. The teacher who marks a six-year-old's essay as good and then returns from seeing a David

Hare play and says it was good, is not suggesting that her six-year-old writes as well as David Hare does; she is using two entirely different scales. A bad poem of Browning or Dyer is not at all the same sort of thing as a bad verse in a greetings card; and a bad passage in Schumann is a long way from the badness of the latest pop single by the England football team.

There are two solutions which seem to offer themselves. The first is to treat all ideas of goodness and badness as pure matters of taste on a level with the I-like-celery-and-you-don't example. There is, therefore, no such thing as bad taste, only different tastes; John Masefield is as good as Shakespeare, the Beatles are as good as Bach. Full stop. But we know this won't do. We feel instinctively that Rembrandt *is* a better artist than my cousin's four-year-old grandson, but this theory gives us no reason to say so. We can find further evidence for distrusting this theory in that though we may like Agatha Christie and like Shake-speare, we do not consider them equivalent. Strangely, we like Shakespeare because of his rich characterization, his rele-vance to our own hopes and failures, his unfathomable lin-guistic inventiveness; and we like Agatha Christie *despite* her cardboard characters, despite her utter irrelevance to anything we have experienced, despite her clichéd diction. In fact the word 'like' seems to be being used in two com-pletely opposed senses. It often is. We say we like our friends and we like dried apricots, but we don't mean the same thing: we would more easily countenance a world without dried apricots than a world without any of our friends.

C. S. Lewis was fascinated by this apparently indefin-able difference between good and bad. He wrote about it at least three times: in an article called 'High and Low Brows' and in 'Different Tastes in Literature', and most fully, towards the end of his life, in a small but convinc-ingly argued book called *An Experiment in Criticism*. It is a book that should not be missed; it can be read in two hours, and I will merely state his conclusions as the other possible solution to the problem.

He notices that books are read in different ways; indeed, that books invite a certain sort of reading. Some while away an idle moment, are tossed aside and never looked at again; others become part of their readers' vision of the world. They are read and reread; they are rolled round the tongue, quoted and discussed with as much energy and excitement as we discuss real people and real places. Bad books, he concludes, are those that invite the first type of reading, and good books are those that invite the second. If we find that a book which we would unhesitatingly place in the first category has been read again and again by even one reader, we must reconsider our judgement. Nobody, he argues, reads a book *because* it is bad: the faults are invisible because they are using the book not for what it is, but for what it suggests. Because, let us say, it is about beautiful people gambling in Monte Carlo and we would rather like to be beautiful people gambling in Monte Carlo, we attend to the day-dreams it arouses in us and not to the book itself. We don't see what is actually there, it merely serves as a kick-start to our fantasies. Good literature is much harder to use in this way. It demands a different sort of attention.

This explains very adequately the Agatha Christie/ Shakespeare problem raised earlier. We read Agatha Christie for the thrill of the chase, the cunning twist which she can engineer quite brilliantly. We read Shakespeare with a different sort of attention. Once we know whodunnit in a Miss Marple story, there is not much of interest in the book; but the power and significance of *Macbeth* does not empty out after a single performance.

The difference between good and bad books can almost be summed up by saying that bad books merely bring out what is already inside us; they pander to us, they indulge us. Good books add something to what we are; they extend us, they change us, they surprise us with more than just a clever plot.

What, I hope, we can also see more clearly now is that there is no kudos attached to being either sort of reader:

there is no insurmountable barrier between the two and most of us combine both sorts quite happily. The reader of bad books will never get beyond himself because bad books do not lead beyond the self; but that self of the bad reader may already be a wiser, purer, greater self than mine even though I read good books. There is no moral turpitude to be imputed to a bad reader, just as there is no moral virtue to be claimed by a good one. But, if it is true that it is good to grow and develop and learn and extend our sympathies and our understanding (all of which I think we can agree with even though it would take another volume to prove it), then we do end up with the expected tautology that good books will be better for us than bad ones. Good books, in other words, do us good; bad books don't do us much good – but that is not the same as saying that they do us harm. We must, though, beware of the addiction that leads to escapism.

Perhaps I should not have used the phrases 'better for us' and 'do us good'. I believe them to be true, but it is a short step from that truth to the erroneous idea that we should read literature in order to improve ourselves. Literature does not give up its real treasures to the status-seeker. The perceived need to be cultured is the true enemy of real enjoyment and understanding of all works of art. Children, as has been pointed out, do put on physical and mental muscle as they play, but it is a by-product. They play because they love playing. Tell a child it's 'good for him' and he'll do his best to stop, because children are more sensible than we are.

Music is music and poetry is poetry, and when either becomes a mere pass-mark in social acceptability we are diminished by them rather than extended.

This was brought home to me recently when I heard a very intelligent interviewer on Radio 3 ask his guest, 'What do you look for in a piece of music?' Now, such a question is not a bad one if it is designed to start a discussion, but it ought to give us a jolt. It implies that music – and we could substitute literature – is a commodity that suits us or does not suit us, something we fit into that crass modern invention, our 'lifestyle'; a kind of fashion accessory. Classic FM is even more brazen about it, talking in terms of 'prestigious' operas. Not good operas, not operas you'll love, not operas you will be challenged or fascinated or moved by, but operas which will lend you prestige should you be seen to attend them. Music to mark yourself by.

The question one should be asking is, 'What does this music look for in me?' For, as Lewis points out, the first step towards a work of art is surrender. Don't impose yourself on it – if you do, you will only find yourself as in a looking-glass – let it impose itself on you; see it for what it is, not for what you can make of it. Then, and only then, will it be able to say to you what its creator wanted you to hear rather than your own trite syllables. Then, and only then, can it shine its lantern into your darkness and illuminate you.

6

A world in a grain of sand *

———⟢———

The fact of our existence precedes any facts about our beliefs. We are humans before we are Christians; we have to have life before we can dogmatize about its meaning and its purpose.

When religion feeds into life and then into writing it can become literature: fiction, poetry, drama. When religion and writing meet outside the boundaries of lived experience you get theology or ethics or dogma, all of which are very different things from literature. Depending on your point of view, they may be more than literature or less, but that is beside the point. The point is that dogma is not literature until it has passed through the chaotic amalgam of doubt, certainty, hope, fear, longing, bewilderment and confusion that we call life. Literature is to do with life; religion is to do with life; and it is life that allows literature (as opposed to non-fiction) to deal with religion.

Literature, as we have seen, is all to do with proving things on our pulses, experiencing them in order fully to understand them. 'Thou shalt not kill' has been the starting-point for a million novels, but only the starting-point. The dogma itself is not literature: only when the novel itself begins to explore why we should not kill, the consequences of murder, the grief and the guilt, the causes, the desires and all the other complexities that surround the act, do we

* Blake: 'Auguries of Innocence'

get literature – *Crime and Punishment* or *The Case of the Addled Oyster*. If you think the latter is likely to be inferior to the former, you may well be right; it's difficult to be sure because it is a made-up title. But beware of despising what appears to be a light genre. The thinking behind any detective story is always to do with the righting of terrible injustice, the restoration of harmony and peace after division and discord. Even a mediocre writer cannot avoid some sense of outraged morality and the possibility of healing if the story is to work as a story. In the hands of a writer such as Ruth Rendell there will also be quite profound psychological truth, and P. D. James fulfils the promise of many of her titles and sets her stories within a specifically Christian understanding of good and evil, right and wrong.

Because literature deals with beliefs filtered through life rather than with the belief itself in pure, dogmatic form, it will be inclined less to state those beliefs than to question them, hold them up to the light. This is not only a valuable process for the Christian, it is a vital one. There is no more pitiable creature than the one who knows it all. When we begin to consider the myriad things we do not, cannot and will never know, even within our own field of expertise, we can begin to see how the rigidity and inflexibility of the know-all is a last-ditch defence for abject fear and insecurity. When this know-all quality is attached to Christian belief it becomes positively dangerous.

To be a Christian is not to assume a position but to begin a process. God is all too often produced, like a rabbit out of a hat, as the answer to all problems, whereas it is probably truer to the experience of a Christian to see God as the source of the problem. After all, if there is really no such thing as ultimate truth, morality, virtue, responsibility or duty, then the problems of life are, at a stroke, reduced to almost nothing, and certainly nothing worth writing about. Ted Hughes puts it succinctly:

> How things are between man and his idea of the
> Divinity determines everything in his life, the quality

and connectedness of every feeling and thought, and the meaning of every action.

(Hughes, *A Choice of Shakespeare's Verse*)

Writers, of course, whether Christians or not, do not carry a kind of sack of beliefs around into which they delve every time they begin a poem or a play. If they have a world-view, it is not to be conceived as a finished article, perfect and complete, which they proceed to illustrate by their writings, though some methods of criticism may help to give this impression. At the end of a life a kind of through-line of belief, a particular kind of engagement with the world, may be discerned in a writer's output and it may interest a critic to trace this distinctive flavour in the various works of the writer; to find where it is barely hinted at, where it is an informing presence, where it flaws the work, where it elevates it. It is only a small step from identifying these ideas to talking of the works as 'embodying' them; as if the poem or the play were written specifically to give voice to the ideas. But, left to themselves, writers do not work like that.

A world-view is less of an objective presence than a constant pressure. It is not something to be worked into every poem, regardless of tact or taste or appropriateness. The good writer is not like the boring friend who will turn every conversation towards football, or the one who always manages to get in a reference to the time when he met Princess Margaret. Writing is not like painting by numbers – put the right words in the right places and you will end up with a picture everyone can recognize. Some bad writing is like that. James Thomson's *The Seasons* is very like painting by numbers, and there is a reason for this. Thomson was writing imitatively at the end of a particular tradition, and this is often where you find the worst poetry. The source of the style he is imitating may have been very strong and reasonable but, like anything else, it became weakened by being imitated again and again. By the time we get to Thomson it is only a shadow of what it was to start with. A kind of Chinese Whispers has taken place.

Thomson is mesmerized by the superficialities of elegant diction and periphrasis, never mind whether it suits his material or not. The result is often laughable, as here in this description of the relaxations of an autumn night (*October* is a kind of ale):

> the mighty bowl
> Swell'd high with fiery juice, steams liberal round
> A potent gale, delicious as the breath
> Of Maia to the love-sick shepherdess,
> On violets diffus'd, while soft she hears
> Her panting shepherd stealing to her arms.
> Nor wanting is the brown *october*, drawn,
> Mature and perfect, from his dark retreat
> Of thirty years; and now his honest front
> Flames in the light refulgent, not afraid
> Even with the vineyard's best produce to vie.
> To cheat the thirsty moments, whist a while
> Walks his grave round, beneath a cloud of smoke,
> Wreath'd fragrant from the pipe; or the quick dice,
> In thunder leaping from the box, awake
> The sounding gammon; while romp-loving miss
> Is haul'd about, in gallantry robust.
>
> (Thomson, 'Autumn', *The Seasons*)

Lengthy quotation is necessary to bring out the true awfulness of the passage: homely games described as if they were Homeric. That passage is very like painting by numbers: the 'correct' words and the correct grave inversions and epic similes – but of course they are not at all correct for the atmosphere he is trying to convey. He has so completely failed to match tone and subject matter that it is tempting to wonder whether he was describing anything that he had ever witnessed or been attracted by.

We started by talking of a world-view and have slipped into a discussion of style, or a defect of style. The two concepts are not unconnected.

The 'correctness' of style in *The Seasons* is the result of Thomson trying to make his work acceptable to a certain sort of audience. The style is a kind of selling strategy, a marketing ploy; in the same way, today's advertisers will stress the ecologically sound nature of their product and its packaging; producers of soap operas will introduce characters from every ethnic and socio-economic background in order to avoid alienating any part of their potential audience.

A world-view, an often undigested lump of philosophy, can, just as speciously, be introduced into a work of literature if the writer is an adherent of some political movement or religious persuasion in order to prove their credentials. If you have a flag you have to wave it.

Never mind that it is intrusive or irrelevant, the Marxist must bring the class-struggle into his poem about the new-born foal; the Christian has to mention the redeeming power of the cross in his short story about the village fishing contest. Out of place, such missionary zeal is self-defeating: it always reduces and often opens to ridicule the very ideas that the author was so anxious to promulgate.

Details of one's philosophy do not have to be explored or thrust to the fore in everything one writes. The pressure of a world-view is felt like a heartbeat: always there but not always present to the conscious mind. It is a kind of background noise to our own internal universe, rather like the echo of creation's big bang that astronomers say they have discovered.

A world-view is seldom what goes into a poem, but it may be what comes out of it. The best kind of philosophy is the product of the poem in the mind of the reader, not the cause of the poem in the mind of the writer; it is discovered not stated; it comes via language and imagery and tone, via the unstated as much as by the stated.

As a writer, you begin by seeing and you end up by saying. Or, at least, you end up with other people saying that you are saying, but it doesn't feel like that to you; it feels much more tentative, much more experimental, much more temporary.

One of the reasons for this is that poetry always begins

with the concrete – the rook on the fence, the candle in the window, the lighthouse – and moves, by means of the poet's own changing vision or the reader's greed for significance in what is before him, towards the general or the universal. An efficient poem does not try to embody the idea 'war is terrible' in poetic form. That may be what the reader sees the poem is 'saying', especially if he is reading the poems of Siegfried Sassoon or Wilfred Owen, when poem after poem responds to a particular death, the sun shining on mingled blood and mire or a gassed soldier howling in agony. The piling up of horror on horror, the great harvest of pain, waste and humiliation is something we become aware of through such poetry, but not in those terms; they are abstracts, and abstracts, even when generally true, to some extent falsify the concreteness of the poem. A poem is always much more complex than any reduction we might make of it in order to describe or catalogue it.

We must always beware of this, because if we approach a poet feeling that we know what he is about, that we have his world-view taped and pigeon-holed, we shall nearly always miss what he is actually giving us. It is so tempting to stick Chesterton in a jar labelled 'bluff, vigorous Christianity', Hardy in another marked 'pessimism' and to bottle and sell Walter de la Mare as 'silvery moonlight, old ruins, memories, etc.' The result is that when you go to them, you go to them thinking that you know what you are going to find – and so that is precisely what you do find, because something of that is certainly there, but it is far from the whole truth and, sometimes, is not the truth at all. The poet has given you a lantern, and all you can see is a looking-glass which reflects back to you your own prejudices, your own inability to allow for surprise, for a pattern to shift. If you look for the confirmation of a prejudice, you will nearly always overlook the particular that will shake that prejudice. Writers are not as tidy as our personal reference system would like them to be.

To dismiss de la Mare because we know all about his silvery ruins and his gentle Georgian diction is to miss the fathomless disquiet of his best work and the subtleties of a diction that has suffered at the hands of inept imitators: Georgian equivalents of James Thomson. The syllogism: 'Georgian poetry is X; de la Mare is a Georgian poet; therefore de la Mare's poetry is X' is reductive to the point of stupidity. Those who would label Hardy as a pessimist owe it to us to explain what he means when, in *Tess of the D'Urbervilles*, he talks of:

The invincible instinct towards self-delight

and

The appetite for joy which pervades all creation, that tremendous force which sways humanity to its purpose.

Or when he writes, at the very end of one of his most tragic novels, *The Mayor of Casterbridge*:

And in being forced to class herself among the fortunate she did not cease to wonder at the persistence of the unforeseen, when the one to whom such unbroken tranquillity had been accorded in the adult stage was she whose youth had seemed to teach that happiness was but the occasional episode in a general drama of pain.

'Seemed' is the important word there: implying that the opposite could be true, *is* in fact true in her experience.

The trouble with a reductive view of literature that would strip down works of art to what we think they 'say' is that one ends up in a cul-de-sac of falsehood, believing that literature is no more than a repetition of a few dozen basic truisms such as: 'We all have to die'; 'I love you and it is wonderful and painful'; 'How beautiful the world is'; and 'What am I doing here?' But the reality is, as anyone who reads will know, that works of literature are not perceived like this at all. Each is unique and, in so far as it is efficiently crafted, is untranslatable. Archibald McLeish's famous poem 'Ars Poetica', ends with the lines:

A poem should not mean
But be

That sounds good until we look closer. In fact those two lines, because of the explicit rational and intellectual statement they contain, contradict the very point they are trying to make. The whole poem has been a kind of argument to convince us that a poem should not be an argument.

I think there is a truth hovering round those two lines, and it is that a poem's being *is* its meaning. Not a choice between being and meaning, but an identification of the two. The being of the poem is its meaning, and nothing in it is superfluous to that meaning. The medium, as has been said in a different context, is the message. That is why the definition of poetry as 'what gets lost in translation' is more than a clever and memorable aphorism – it identifies the poem's meaning as inseparable from the actual words and forms that the poet has deliberately and consciously used.

It is not dodging the issue to say that a poem cannot be fully explained; it is to state a truth of the same order as to say that infinity cannot fully be measured. A measurable infinity is no infinity at all: a paraphrasable poem is no poem at all. If you doubt that, take what might at first sight appear to be a very simple poetic utterance – the Edward Thomas poem 'Thaw', which we considered in the previous chapter, or a short lyric by one of the masters of that form, Robert Frost – and try to contain all that it means to you in a different form with different words. It's a bit like trying to catch the wind in a string bag. It's not a game you can win, but it does help you to see what kind of skill and sensibility has gone into making such a piece of work; and it will help towards an understanding of the difference between creativity which has behind it an entire lifetime of authority and experience and vision involving the whole person, and mere reproduction or mouthing of matters of passing interest.

This is why W. H. Auden in his day-dream College for Bards described in his essay 'The Poet and the City' would ban his students from reading or writing any literary criticism as such and require of them only the writing of parodies. And by parody he means parody and not burlesque. Burlesque deals with a specific poem and pokes fun by changing the theme:

> Twinkle, twinkle little bat!
> How I wonder what you're at!
> Up above the world you fly,
> Like a teatray in the sky.

It calls for neither wit nor skill and is usually pretty pointless. Parody, however, demands a genuine and deep understanding of the way in which the mind of the person being parodied works. It involves asking why he does this, how he manages that – precisely the sort of questions a good critic would try to answer. But Auden preferred parody to a prose critique because the parody is criticism incarnate, criticism made flesh and therefore more immediate and more powerful; just as Christ becomes more immediate and powerful when he ceases to be a theological reference point and becomes Christ incarnate, a man.

What we have been saying about literature – the uniqueness of a poem that, like a person, is not duplicable, the way in which it *is* itself rather than limits itself merely to saying or standing for, the way in which it points to the philosophical by way of the concrete rather than the other way around – can be summed up by saying that literature itself is incarnational. It gets involved. It engages itself with the grime of existence and lived experience rather than with the pure ether of theoretical logic. It is untidily real and disturbingly, sometimes distressingly, inquisitive. It can strip the skin off our preconceptions and reveal to us that what we perhaps considered eternal is only provisional; it can help us to face what we do not understand and, in doing so, lead us to a greater understanding.

And most readers will agree, so long as it is implied that we are dealing with poems, novels and plays written by Christians; people who see the world in very much the same terms as we do ourselves. But this is to look at the matter the wrong way round. We must judge a writer not by what we deem his beliefs to be, but by what we learn from the works themselves. You can't decide who is a good potter until you have seen his pots. An archbishop is as capable of writing anodyne twaddle as an atheist is of straight talking. We came by our beliefs, whatever they may be, by testing them against our knowledge, our experience, our deepest feelings and emotions, and we must test literature in the same way. There is at least one novelist who makes no secret of his Christianity and whose novels are a tissue of half-truths from beginning to end; hysterical, unbalanced, ill-conceived and dangerous. I would give all his works for a single poem from that miserable old atheist, Thomas Hardy, and I would be the healthier for it. Christians do not have a monopoly on truth or integrity.

As I hope has been made clear, generalizations are dangerous – mainly because they cannot admit the exceptions that we tend, now, to find more interesting and significant than the rule they conflict with – but the majority of English literature, even through the Enlightenment, so called, and up to the Victorian age, has been written from a Christian understanding. Even those, such as George Eliot, who argued with Christianity knew very well what they were arguing with. It is when we come to the end of the nineteenth century and into the twentieth that we find that the argument, as such, has ceased and Christianity begins to be ignored rather than actually opposed. The -isms begin to proliferate: Marxism, existentialism, humanism, structuralism, and so forth.

What we must admit to ourselves before we begin to dismiss them as of no interest to us is that no one ever wrote a book which was meant to be dishonest or wrong-headed or beguilingly untruthful. Nor was any philosophy held for the sake of it, but because the holder believed it to be true. It behoves us to take seriously those who will have nothing to do with any sort of theistic or specifically Christian belief, because, although they will offer what must seem to the believer partial or wrong-headed answers (supposing they offer them at all), they will be asking the difficult questions; the questions we ourselves must address if our creed is to be more than a mere formula. They may not have found any light, or if they have it may only be a flickering candle flame, but they are liable to have seen the same terrifying darkness as we have.

Paradoxically, the humanist and existentialist see man as much more noble and heroic than the Christian, without being able to give any inkling of where that nobility or heroism comes from, or even how it is defined. The Christian can see how man may become noble and heroic, though his definition of the qualities will be rather different from that of the atheist in many regards, but he sees man as the problem rather than the innocent sufferer ('slighted and enduring' in the words of Hardy) in a world devoid of meaning. The Christian does not believe that man can pull himself up by his own bootstraps; the pagan in all his various affiliations believes that man *can* pull himself up, but has nowhere to pull himself to. The most that all his social, political and intellectual action can do for him is make him 'aware'. But if he cannot do anything to change what he becomes aware of, we are justified in asking what point there was in his becoming aware in the first place. It might be better for a man locked in a prison from which there is no escape not to be aware of the fact. It might lessen his pain. But then, it depends what you mean by 'better', and the pagan has only a very woolly answer to that question.

He will probably be right in his call for justice and freedom and the abolition of false values, in his call for the reassessment of motives and pretentions and ideals; but while he would want to change the world for man's sake, the Christian would want to change man, for the world's sake and for his own. Or, to put it a different way, if we imagine an out and out pagan and an out and out Christian – and we may have to imagine them, for they occur less frequently than one might think – the former would generally be heard claiming rights and freedom while the latter would be issuing reminders about duties and respon- sibilities. But, of course, the two go hand in hand: one man's right is another's duty, one man's freedom rests on another's responsibility.

In dealing theoretically with such matters we have already slipped into a way of talking about literature as if it were a means of illustrating a philosophy. It is always easier to talk about a work of art in terms of sociology, morality, history or philosophy than it is to talk about it as art. The alternative is to discuss it only in terms of pattern and diction and craft. We have been led into this difficulty by the fact that we are dealing with language, with the fact that the elements that go to make up the art of literature have meaning in and of themselves. This is not true of any other art.

An F# in music has no meaning; nor does the chord of D major in which it may be found. A blob of green or white, a line or a curve in graphic art, has no meaning in itself. A movement in dance has no intrinsic meaning, though if it is repeated often enough in similar contexts it will gather significance and may, for those who have seen enough, become part of a fairly limited vocabulary of movement. When we talk of the 'meaning' of a symphony or a painting by Rothko or a non-narrative ballet, we are on shaky ground and are at the mercy of our own memories and subjective impressions. Stravinsky agreed that music is, in essence, meaningless, and here is another composer, Paul Hindemith:

> Sometimes in southern countries church music can be heard which for the visitor from the North has the most exhilarating effect, although it may be intended as funeral music and will have the proper effect of such on the native listener . . .
>
> I like to mention the second movement of Beethoven's Seventh Symphony, which I have found leads some people into a pseudo feeling of profound

melancholy, while another group takes it for a kind of scurrilous scherzo, and a third for a subdued pastorale. Each group is justified in judging as it does

(Hindemith, A Composer's World, ch. 3)

The 'meaning' which we superimpose on these abstract works of art is a mixture of subjective memory and available emotion, along with a perception of the structure and the patterning of the whole.

But literature is different. The elements that go to make it up are in themselves meaningful. Verbs and nouns carry the most meaning, adjectives and adverbs slightly less; but even conjunctions, pronouns, articles and prepositions are definable. We cannot escape some kind of philosophical content in literature, and it tends to overshadow all other considerations, which is why I have been at pains to stress that there is much more to it than this; that literature as an art must also be seen in terms of form and pattern and rhythm and arrangement; that the true meaning of a poem or a novel is bound up in the very words and shapes that appear on the page. True literature is, in this respect, music as well as mimesis.

If we are to communicate anything of interest to one another when we talk of a 'good' poem or a good novel, this must be kept in mind. A poem is not to be called good simply because it feeds us ideas and opinions we like to hear, any more than a driver should be considered good because he has arrived where he wanted to be, even though he has killed three people on the way, knocked down a fence and ruined his gearbox.

Nor, truly, can we talk of a good sonnet merely because it has fulfilled the demands of the sonnet's form and rhyme-scheme if the subject matter is banal, unintelligible or repugnant. Our metaphorical driver would then be someone who kept his car beautifully polished and maintained, but had nowhere to go in it. Even though we may have to separate form and content when we come to analyse or discuss a work of literature, true excellence will reside in the poem where the two cannot be disentangled without damage or misunderstanding. When we meet such a poem our instinctive desire is not to take it apart, not to try and explain the miracle, but simply to read it again.

In purely literary terms, judgements about a book's morality are neither here nor there; a flawless novel or poem may be written that promulgates a world-view that we would reject. This is the area where literature can – not necessarily 'does' – become dangerous. Because of the way in which the story is told, we accept it. It may be that it is administering a poison to our bloodstream, but if the injection is painless or even pleasurable, we accept the drug.

In all humility we must keep our literary judgements separate from those that we make as Christians. We may, as critics, point out what we have discovered by reading a book – maybe that the way the author has used language or employed a certain structure of images shows that he is subtly pulling us into assumptions and a framework of belief that we did not start out with and that we would repudiate if we were conscious of it. As G. K. Chesterton says:

> The morality of a great writer is not the morality he teaches, but the morality he takes for granted,
> (Chesterton, 'The Superstition of Divorce')

and it is certainly our job as critics to lay bare that framework, to demonstrate how the sleight of hand is effected. About the belief itself – whether we agree or disagree with it – the literary critic as such will have nothing to say. It is not the literary critic's place to say that Christianity is true, or false. He may show how it is both genesis and hindrance in a work such as *Paradise Lost* or *The Divine Comedy*, but as soon as he ventures a judgement on its universal truth or falsehood he is in the realm of religion, ethics, philosophy. No one will deny him an opinion in such matters, but he must not think that his distinction as a critic makes that opinion any more valuable.

That is why we shall find so much aesthetic and so little morality in the critics we read when they are writing for a general audience. Whether Sartre's novel is or is not a true work of art does not depend on his ideas, unless they can be shown to be ideas that are not conducive to a good novel; it depends rather on what he has done with them, how he has invested them in character and in action, what significance they have in the world he has invented and described and how vividly he makes them appeal to us. When we have described all that, we have done with the work of art. Then we may, if we wish, carry on to consider its eternal value and truth.

But we must remember on what terms we understand the truth. In absolute terms we are never going to grasp it. We are used to hearing in our law courts a promise to tell 'the truth, the whole truth and nothing but the truth'. Applied to mere motivation and memory, that is hard enough; when it comes to understanding the universe and all that lies behind it, it is an impossible concept. We can aim at the truth, we can aim at nothing but the truth as we have perceived it, but the whole truth is not attainable. If we are aware of this limitation, we shall be less impatient with those who see a different kind of truth from ourselves and not be afraid to inspect our own truths in the light of theirs. We need not be afraid. The truth will bear any amount of testing if it is the truth, and if it is not, the sooner that is discovered the better. Only fear and false pride refuses to be tested.

We can admit within the church, within what we call the body of Christ, many differences of balance, opinion, experience, interpretation; we are all at different stages on the road. We should be able to extend that sympathy beyond the church and into the world.

What the world likes to think of Christians is not true: they are not automata or clones or puppets fastened to the strings of determinism. They may dance to the same tune, but their steps are gloriously different, and so is the shape of each individual's dance. To be a Christian is not to be assimilated into some kind of vague divinity, some benevolent New Age force, but to make discovery of who we

really are. It is not a blurring but a focusing. Most important of all, it is a movement forward, not a stasis; it is
more to do with what we can become than with what we
are already. So in literature we should not look for dogma,
for a closed philosophical system or a kind of pigeon-
holing, but a reaching out, a tasting, a trying, a daring and
questioning. It is only shaky, fearful, temporal secular
institutions that will not allow questions. 'Don't rock the
boat' and 'Toe the party line' are orders that are needed
only when the institution is vulnerable. The truth is not
vulnerable.

What image comes to mind when you read that most
famous passage in the teaching of Jesus:

> And Jesus called a little child unto him, and set him in
> the midst of them, and said, Verily I say unto you,
> Except ye be converted, and become as little children,
> ye shall not enter into the kingdom of heaven.
>
> (Matt. 18. 2–3)

What qualities was Jesus expecting us to display in our
becoming like little children? One of the things we have
already noted about children is their capacity for wonder,
for being continually open to surprise and delight. That is
true enough, and is probably what most people consider
Jesus was referring to in this passage. But there is another
very distinctive quality about children, perhaps the most
distinctive of all, and to ignore it is to imply that Jesus did
not understand children or to admit that you know very
little about them. What I am thinking of is their insatiable
curiosity, their constant questioning of everything. They
are relentless explorers, avid for information and experience.
Who? What? Where? When? How? Why? Why? Why?
Why? That is what children are like. Ask any parent. They
weary you with their energy and their questions. It is
this quality, above all, that adults lose, and this quality –
not unmixed with wonder and innocence, which are all
part of it – that I am convinced was in Jesus' mind when

he recommended a childlike approach to life if we are to discover the kingdom and be given its freedom.

We question ourselves, of course, and, as readers, we allow others to look at this complex web of creation in all its beauty and all its corruption and ask their own questions. What we demand of literature is not that it should offer some Christian view of life but that, at the very least, it does not fudge the facts, that it does not lie about human behaviour – even by omission – and that it does not sentimentalize or over-simplify. Answers are difficult for literature because the best stories are not logical syllogisms or moral philosophy, but they should be asking the right questions without denying aspects of our humanity.

We should also remember that although Auden talked of poems never being finished, only abandoned, once they appear in black and white on the page they do give every sign of being finished. They stand like a monument; but they are only a moment's monument. Life goes on, new explorations are made; the poem has been abandoned in the search for a deeper or a more lasting way of putting things. The writer's voice gets richer, his experience deepens, what was, at the time, nothing but the truth is now seen clearly as far from the whole truth. But the poem stands, unchanged, as a kind of reproach. There is nothing we can do about this as readers. We can only discuss what exists and remember that every work of art is a provisional, temporary truth until time proves it worth preserving and it takes its place as a true facet of the whole truth.

There is a breathtakingly arrogant remark of George Bernard Shaw's which is not a million miles from many a Christian attitude to literature. He wrote:

> With the single exception of Homer, there is no eminent writer, not even Sir Walter Scott, whom I can despise so entirely as I despise Shakespeare when I measure my mind against his.
>
> (Shaw, *Dramatic Opinions and Essays*, vol. 2)

which is explained, though not entirely justified, by G. K. Chesterton:

> The point was that he could not, in all sincerity, see what the world saw in Homer or Shakespeare, because what the world saw was not what G. B. S. was then looking for. He was looking for that ghastly thing which Nonconformists call a Message, and continue to call a Message, even when they have become atheists and do not know who the Message is from. He was looking for a system.
>
> (Chesterton, Chaucer, ch. 1)

And all too often the Christian will make the same mistake: he will be searching for a message, a system of which he can approve (or one of which he can securely disapprove) rather than a prospect or a challenge or even a truthful reflection of the ambiguities and ambivalences of life as man perceives it.

The looking-glass is safe: it reflects to us the images we are comfortable with, the world we know; but the lantern may guide our feet, even if it is along a difficult path, into lands full of light and truth.

7

Brimful of moral[*]

———

When we are discussing a work of literature we must account everything as relevant, just as, from the point of view of God, every tiny stimulus, every thought, every nudge that the world gives us is relevant to the way our lives are shaped. For a full understanding we must miss out as little as possible. Something, inevitably, will be missed out or given the wrong emphasis simply because we cannot fully share the perceptions and the sensibilitites of anyone else. Granted that the novel or the poem is the very means by which the author is attempting to share his perceptions, there will still be a shortfall which is due to blind spots in our psychological make-up, differing experiences of the subject of work – or no experience at all – and all the weight of thought and personal opinion that combine to make us who we are rather than who the author is. This, of course, is where the imagination comes in. The imagination can work on a good piece of writing with very happy results, but it will never quite make up for a lack of relevant experience. But then, the point of the poem or the novel or the play is to push us towards understanding an experience which we may never have had.

Anyone, for instance who has never had a child will be differently moved (not perhaps *less* moved) by Jon Silkin's

* W. S. Landor: 'Lines to a Dragon Fly'

poem 'Death of a Son', Anthony Thwaite's 'Sick Child' and Ben Jonson's 'On My First Son', from someone who has had a child; and, almost certainly, that person will be differently moved from someone who has actually lost a child. The quality of the poem is such as to be moving in itself; we all understand the dreadful division that death makes, and most of us have experienced it. Those memories, emotions and sympathies are revived when we read about a death we have not experienced.

You do not need to have climbed Snowdon at night to be captivated by Wordsworth's description of the experience:

> For instantly a light upon the turf
> Fell like a flash, and lo! as I looked up,
> The Moon hung naked in a firmament
> Of azure without cloud, and at my feet
> Rested a silent sea of hoary mist.
> A hundred hills their dusky backs upheaved
> All over this still ocean; and beyond,
> Far, far beyond, the solid vapours stretched
> In headlands, tongues and promontory shapes,
> Into the main Atlantic, that appeared
> To dwindle, and give up his majesty,
> Usurped upon as far as the sight could reach.
> Not so the ethereal vault; encroachment none
> Was there, nor loss; only the inferior stars
> Had disappeared, or shed a fainter light
> In the clear presence of the full-orbed Moon,
> Who, from her sovereign elevation, gazed
> Upon the billowy ocean as it lay
> All meek and silent . . .
>
>   (Wordsworth, *The Prelude*, bk. 14, 38–56)

Nor do you have to have been brought up in a country cottage to appreciate the powerful beauty of this:

> Whether the summer clothe the general earth
> With greenness, or the redbreast sit and sing
> Betwixt the tufts of snow on the bare branch

Of mossy apple-tree, while the nigh thatch
Smokes in the sun-thaw; whether the eve-drops fall
Heard only in the trances of the blast,
Or if the secret ministry of frost
Shall hang them up in silent icicles,
Quietly shining to the quiet moon.

(Coleridge, 'Frost at Midnight')

I have not climbed Snowdon, but I was brought up in a country cottage among hills, and I have seen the sights described in these two poems; seen them so often, indeed, that I find it difficult to understand why I find both passages so moving and so emotionally exciting. The only answer I can come up with is that there are some experiences that are valuable in and of themselves; experiences that point to something that answers very deeply to certain of our psychological needs. When we cannot find them, we are impoverished, and whenever we do meet them, whether it be in Sussex or whether it be given pattern and significance at the climax of a poem, we are enriched and satisfied. We find enjoyment and fulfilment in being shown what we already know as well as what only the poet could give form to and communicate to us. We are in touch again with something we did not know we lacked, that we did not know was important until the poet showed it to us.

This is true not only of nature, but of love and death and of every tiny emotion that touches us. Nothing is insignificant. Gratefully we clasp hands with a poet who may have lived a century ago or five centuries ago: he has helped to show us who we are and how – as John Donne said – we are involved with mankind. His lantern swings across our sometimes cloudy looking-glass and illuminates the world of memory and joy, of pain and truth and sheer being that we share with him.

If literature has any value, it is because our life and our humanity has value. Every insight into that life is useful, is challenging, nourishing or consoling. The insight can come through the sudden perception of pattern and meaning discovered in a metaphor or verbal device; it can come through ethics or metaphysics or morality or a world-view subtly adrift from our own, for literature combines all these elements. Literature is a compound, not an element; an alloy, not a pure metal. We shall always be disappointed if we go to it for instruction. We must not be sure of what we want to find, but ready to be argued with, extended or surprised. We must surrender. The only way to learn about swimming is to jump into the water; the only way to fly is to get into the aeroplane and trust the pilot. We shall never know whether swimming is good for us or not while we pace, shivering, up and down the sides of the pool.

I hope enough has been said by now about the importance of seeing any piece of writing as a whole, irreducible and interdependent in all its modes of meaning for us to pick out some aspects for further inspection without appearing to deny that principle. If we want to know more about the fish, it sometimes has to be pulled out of the water.

The first thing we should remind ourselves of is a point we have already noted: that what we may hold as immovable precepts can only work in literature when they are, as it were, discovered, proved in action. If moral precepts appear in literature at all, they are embodied; and, because we are dealing with human beings, they are not going to be pure. A man may be drawn as courageous, but he will not always be courageous, nor will he easily be courageous, nor will his courage always prevail. If it were not so, we would not be dealing with anything at all lifelike, but with mere pipe-dreams. We know what perfection is, but we are not perfect. That is the realm of literature: the problem of attaining an ideal in circumstances far from ideal.

'Love one another,' says Jesus. Should we then expect literature to show us people all loving one another? It would have very little to do with any life we know or any people we are acquainted with. We may believe that God is all-powerful, but to write a play in which a gin-soaked foul-mouthed harridan suddenly at the end of the third act drops the knife with which she is about to stab her son and asks Jesus into her life is a travesty of art's integrity. Unfortunately such pieces are written by and approved by vacuous Christians who refuse to see the difference between what God can do and what he will do. They are much more guilty of peddling a false view of life than the honest pagan who is struggling with the truth and looking honestly and without any axe to grind at what the world is like. A Christian who finds he had to lie about his experience in order to defend his God is a dangerous fool and, probably, not much of a Christian.

The Bible may give us the 'right' answer to the sum we are trying to solve, but literature is the working out; and, as your teacher always insisted, we need to see the working out in order to validate the answer. The working out is what proves the understanding.

Why should we expect literature to be any more genteel or comfortable than the Bible? The Bible is about hatred, lies, corruption, lust, broken promises, prostitution, murder, adultery, pride, rape, war, torture, deformity, military occupation, famine, unbelief, fratricide, voyeurism, ignorance, injustice, slavery, drunkenness, rebellion, incest, madness, disease, the occult, revenge, conspiracy, abuse of power, betrayal, greed, envy, racial hatred and death. Because of this it is even more powerfully about love and truth and honesty, friendship, courage, childbirth, dancing, eating, drinking, laughter, simplicity, presents, repentance, endurance, chastity, faithfulness, trust, self-sacrifice, bread, wine, music, consolation, renewal, forgiveness, passion, beauty, justice, peace, humility, miracles, lilies, children, freedom, sleep, poetry, honey, gold, prayer and angels.

Good writing that deals with the truth about mankind does not ignore the dunghill. Some writers get rather too attracted by the dunghill; they bury themselves in it up to the neck, so that their vision is limited to that of the dunghill, and they talk about dung, dung, dung. That's not enough. But there are some writers who float, piously, a couple of feet above the dunghill and refuse to admit that it is there waiting for them. That's not enough, either; such writers avoid the blinkered vision of the first type, but they avoid also even that measure of genuine truth and, since they haven't got their feet on the ground, have nothing but the airy-fairy to balance it with. The true writer is the one who has his feet firmly on the dunghill from where he can get a very good view of the stars.

We must always distinguish between an indulgence in evil and a taking into account of evil. That fine writer Dennis Potter has been responsible for a number of intelligent, crafted and challenging plays guaranteed to provoke argument and thought among people of every kind of political or religious persuasion. But he was not immune to indulgence. He defended his film *Blackeyes* as an exposé of how men treat women as sex objects. It was certainly defensible as such, but only theoretically. What he was 'saying' was in many ways at odds with what he was allowing us to see. Now, in chapter 1 of this book, I warned that to ignore or overlook sinfulness is to diminish the depth of the forgiveness or the repentance, and I stick to that principle. But there is a line, sometimes very fine, between allowing the sinfulness its proper power and starting to enjoy portraying it for its own sake. Most of the public, even if they will not go so far as to admit the fact openly, are not disinclined to watch naked men and women – particularly women – on film or television, nor will they skip the sex scenes in a novel. It becomes very easy for the writer to start enjoying the activity which he purports to be showing only to condemn it. The balance goes, and what was argued as a defence of morality becomes, in practice, a show of immorality – made, of course, very attractive.

No, a writer can't help anyone unless he knows the problem, but we have to hold in tension our mere humanity and our new humanity, avoiding indulgence on the one hand and glibness on the other. There is a difference between admitting to something and dwelling on it, though to decide when the one becomes the other is likely to be a very subjective judgement. Potter, presumably, really did believe he was laying bare a problem in *Blackeyes*, even though a good number of people thought he was laying bare a cast of attractive women and enjoying it.

The physical world, stubborn, real and law-abiding, is there for all to see and experience, and the basic assumption of all science is that we see it and experience it in very much the same way. Even those who subscribe to the philosophy that objects do not exist unless we are looking at them are not really surprised when the wall they built yesterday remains built today. Even those who subscribe to Bishop Berkeley's theory of the non-existence of matter seem to suspend their beliefs when driving on the motorway, unless a number of philosophical accidents on the M25 has gone unreported.

We accept the 'givenness' of the physical world; its forms and habits are not a matter of opinion. We would disbelieve anyone who said he had seen a blue tree unless we knew he had been in Salvador Dali's garden. We would be surprised if hollies shed their leaves, we do not have to think to ourselves, 'Ah, Wednesday: that means gravity will be working.'

The same is true of the moral universe. It has always been good to be gentle, to be just, unselfish, humble, trustworthy, honest and courageous; it has always been bad to be bullying, unjust, greedy, arrogant, cruel, irresponsible, dishonest and cowardly. That is, if you like to put it that way, the givenness of morality, and the Christian has no unique claim to it. Plenty of people who deny Christ do not deny humility, justice and honesty; they may well exhibit more of it than many a Christian.

But Christianity is more than just moral behaviour. It is at once subtler and more definite than that. This is not the place to go into an analysis of Christian doctrine: most of my readers will be acquainted with it, and those who are not would do better to find a book on the subject or a clergyman to argue with. All I am concerned with here is to point out that there is a difference between something that is specifically *Christian* and something which does not

conflict with the Christian belief. The virtues that I out-
lined above – trustworthiness, humility, unselfishness, and
so forth – are what the Christian would see as by-products
of the life of Christ within him, not ends but results. They
don't conflict with his beliefs, but they don't define them
either. The agnostic thinks God will love him because he
is good; the Christian thinks God will make him good
because God loves him.

I have heard plenty of books and plays described as
Christian, when what was really meant was promulgating
a certain morality; calling for justice, or awakening responsibility, or defending freedom. All of this the Christian
will applaud and approve; where he may differ is in respect
of the way in which such things may be brought about.
What he should always be grateful for is a truthful facing
of the issues, an unswerving honesty in understanding
what it means to be human and to make choices, and an
unsentimental view of man's capacity for self-deception on
the one hand and extraordinary perseverance on the other.
The Christian will welcome the truth even when it is not
the whole truth.

Such literature will seldom be comfortable in the way
that a cathedral evensong is comfortable, because evensong
is about reconciliation and literature is about conflict, even
when that conflict ends, like Milton's *Samson Agonistes*, in

calm of mind, all passion spent.

But it was the peace*makers* whom Christ called blessed in
the Sermon on the Mount, not the peace-*lovers*. The distinction I am making is between those who look for a quiet
life, sweep things under the carpet, paper over the cracks
and turn a blind eye – all clichés that are as easy to write as
they are to fulfil – and those who are active rather than
passive, who, at personal risk, actually face the issues, get
their hands dirty and dare to do something dangerous in
order that peace may be achieved not just assumed. As
Hotspur says in *Henry IV*

out of this nettle danger, we pluck this flower, safety.

A merely pretty literature, all pattern, all aesthetics, all play and no work, would be a waste of time. A voice without a vision is not literature; but neither is a vision without a voice. That is not to say that mere fun, mere entertainment, some delightful piece of froth cannot take its place as one ingredient of a literature. But literature may need more of a backbone than that if it is to be considered in any way important. A life of feasting with friends would not make a very impressive CV, but feasting with friends after hard work is an excellent thing. Life and literature may be serious, but they don't always have to be solemn. The sensible Christian usually understands this and, indeed, finds plenty of reason for laughter in his philosophy. It is usually the agnostic or the pagan moralist who is gloomy and keeps on banging the table.

Morality and Christianity are not the same thing, then, but there is a great deal of overlap between them, and where writers fall short of professing Christianity they will still, if they are true to an honest analysis of our existence, be able to offer insights and conclusions that Christians can both applaud and profit by.

We constantly make divisions in our thinking which, although they are useful temporarily, all too easily become fixed: a momentary contrast becomes an eternal antithesis. So we speak of the English-speaking world and the non-English-speaking world, almost as if the latter were as homogeneous as the former, and clearly it is not. We talk of smokers and non-smokers as if the latter group were able to be typified or defined by their non-doing of something. It is hard enough to classify people positively by what they *do* do, or support or believe, but those who don't do it are not classifiable. The contrast makes it sound as if they are. What, then, when we come to talk of Christians and non-Christians? It's admissible to group people in terms of their belief because that is positive; but the term 'non-Christian' tells us nothing. For dinner tonight we are having non-grass and non-curtains. Helpful terminology, isn't it? That is why I have tended to use the word 'pagan' whenever I want to refer to someone who has no Christian belief. At least it is a positive, robust word which, I hope, carries no implicit criticism.

But there are two huge divisions which I want to look at. They are divisions in history which are echoed in the way we think. For some people one is more important than the other, and for others, one of the divisions is entirely specious and need not to be taken into consideration. This has a great effect on the way both sorts of people write and judge literature.

The first of these divisions is that between before the fall and after the fall, between innocence and experience; the second is that between BC and AD, Old Testament and New Testament, pre-Christian and Christian.

For the Christian, both divisions are real and important, but the second is probably the more important since it supersedes and overturns the first. The incarnation is a response to the problem of the fall; Christ is the second Adam. In a sense Christ is the solution to the problem, but more in the sense of a signpost than of a sticking-plaster. Redemption is a process and not a fact. So, to summarize: the first division is true, and that is why we have a problem; the second division is true, and that is why we have the possibility of a solution. The whole truth is a balance between the two which can be seen and imaged in all sorts of ways – between darkness and light, despair and hope, emptiness and fullness, death and life.

The pagan, on the other hand, will see the second division as a purely imaginary one. Not that he won't perhaps respond, as someone like Shelley did, to the person of Jesus who remains, even for many out and out atheists, a very attractive and unusual figure. But he cannot see him as the Christ. He was a man, and maybe a rather extraordinary man with something important to teach us, but he has no relevance to our predicament at the end of the twentieth century; he may have said things to us, but he can do nothing for us, and all the talk of death and resurrection and salvation is either feeble and ignoble or else it is Christianity mixing its metaphors and getting into a muddle with truth and symbol, image and reality.

What the pagan will, however, admit is the idea of the fall, because he can't really avoid it. Man's dreams are at odds with reality. Life seems to promise one thing and then, so often, delivers another. Our spirit is often out of step with our minds and our bodies. Perfection dances before us like a will-o'-the-wisp, but we can never grasp it. Ideals crowd upon us and, just as soon, melt away again. We entertain great notions of achieving the grand abstract virtues and we fail again and again. Something is wrong; we cannot escape the feeling that this is not how it was meant to be.

Now, all that is true; and the Jew and the Christian would agree with it. That is what the literature of the secular man is bent on exploring and trying to explain. It is all the truth that is left to him if he finds himself unable to accept the work of Christ. But at least it is truth.

The form and dynamic of literary work, Christian and pagan, tragic and comic, seems to shape itself and derive from the narratives of Eden and after. We begin with a state of harmony which is followed by a fall, then there is a transformation and regeneration and then (depending whether it is tragedy or comedy) an end in tears or laughter. This is the shape of all fictions and is as true of *Dennis the Menace* and *Just William* as it is of *King Lear* and *Darkness Visible*. It is an echo of that primal myth – whether you accept it as true or not – that formed our consciousness.

Stories and poems are a proper and incessant refuge for us: a counterpoint to our struggle, an alternative, a sense of the wonderful-impossible – or impossible-at-the-moment, or impossible-in-this-respect. Stories and poems are a mode of belief and assertion in the face of overwhelming odds and outside pressure to give in.

True belief does the same thing, but it still needs the stories just as a burning coal needs the fire beneath it or it will flicker and go out. It holds up justice in the face of injustice, it clings to pattern in the face of the random, consolation in the depths of misery, and holds itself out to possibilities constantly denied by the disappointment of daily experience. It can see the green leaves of spring on the bare winter boughs, and a sea of corn on brown, puddled fields of dock and thistle.

In its best moments a secular society will even admit that it needs some kind of invasion from the outside. Zanna Beswick noted this in a paper given to the International Consultancy on Religion, Education and Culture in 1995:

> There's a journey towards self-knowledge, a reaching for revelation, or perhaps simply for rescue. We may even see that in our insatiable hunger for police and medical series on television: *Casualty*, *Medics*, *Heartbeat*, *The Bill*, *Between the Lines*, *Peak Practice*, *Morse* . . . and I could go on endlessly.

That idea of rescue is a fascinating and entirely plausible one; we need rescuing from our human situation. Once we would have gone to religion for solace and salvation, now we go to men in blue uniforms or white coats. They offer a very practical kind of rescue, especially since we tend to see all our ills in terms of crime or disease; but, interestingly, there is also a kind of mystery about both the detective and the doctor. Medical science is so advanced and complex that no layman can honestly say he understands it. *Casualty* affects us like magic or like the simplest kind of religious impulse: we bring our broken selves to the priests and priestessess of this temple and, on television at least, there is healing and, often, reconciliation.

In the same way, the policeman has powers and stamina far exceeding our own. Like God, he sees through the surface of things into the human heart; he understands motives, rejects falsehood, pierces the darkness and in the end, unerringly, points the finger of justice. We worship him. It is quite telling, too, that the Great Detective usually inhabits a rarefied world far from the common haunts of men, and we revere him all the more for that; he is not like us. So, P. D. James' Adam Dalgleish is a poet and Michael

Innes' Appleby can solve crimes by an esoteric knowledge of art or literature; Morse is an expert in opera and classical music, Simon Brett's Charles Paris takes us backstage in the theatre world of glamour and make-believe, Holmes has his abstruse sciences, Lord Peter Wimsey has everything: unlimited money, access to the highest in the land, a priceless library and a richly stocked mind which is never at a loss for long and a manservant who has a perfectly complementary expertise and circle of friends.

Once we looked for a Messiah; now we put our faith in the hospital and the forces of law and order, whether official or unofficial. And look what happens when we don't get the perfect salvation that we have come to expect from such godlike beings: we sue. We cannot accept human error or accident or overwork or simple failure. If these people are gods, they could have saved us and they didn't. No wonder we are angry. Gods should answer prayer.

Literature is always connected to the world from which it is born; it may be a portrait of that world as the author perceives it, warts and all; or it may be a counterpoint, a rehearsing of different possibilities. Those who see beyond the temporal and into the eternal, whether they are Christians or not, may believe the first method to be immoral or, at the very least, partial, only half the story. And they may well be right. Since literature has no function, as such, or perhaps it would be truer to say that literature may have any of a dozen different functions, it is difficult to make such a judgement. What we can say is that the literature that has endured, the literature that is loved for itself and not just for its significance as a historical document, is the literature that moves us, that we go back to time and time again. Perhaps some of us do need to be told how difficult, intractable and dark life is, and we must not entirely despise the books that tell us that without falsifying the evidence. But what most of us respond to is hope and delight. We respond to the stormy landscape, but how much more do we respond when the sun breaks through and the birds take up their song again.

Most art that has earned itself the epithet 'great' has a decent helping of what Hardy called 'the invincible instinct towards self-delight' in it. And so it should. We will have life and we will have it more abundantly, despite the darkness. Our fallen nature is not yet so fallen that it cannot perceive beauty, cannot yearn, cannot praise. The very act of making a poem or writing a novel is a refusal to be engulfed. A writer cannot, logically, write a poem which concludes that nothing matters. Presumably his poem matters or he would not have bothered to write it. But if his poem matters, then something matters. So if his poem is true, then it is untrue. In other words, if we truly lived in a meaningless world we would be prevented from realizing it, and certainly from saying so, because to say truly that something is meaningless is to mean something and therefore to destroy your thesis at the very moment you form it.

The very existence of literature is a hint to us that meaning is more than a mere desire and truth more than a mere chimera. Just as our physical thirst implies that somewhere there is water, so our spiritual and mental hunger for meaning and pattern, while not proving anything, at least implies the possibility of satisfaction. What kind of creature evolves such a complex and winsome art as literature if it is entirely and demonstrably spurious?

The difficulty, for those who would take a moral view of literature, is to decide where spuriousness might take over from the truth the poet is attempting to pin down. Once language becomes the medium by which sensations are structured and transmitted, there is room for all kinds of ambivalence and ambiguity both in the writing and in the reading. Keats found this of great concern:

The Imagination may be compared to Adam's dream – he awoke and found it truth. I am the more zealous in this affair, because I have never yet been able to perceive how any thing can be known for truth by consequitive reasoning ... However it may be, O for

a Life of Sensations rather than of Thoughts!
(Keats, letter to Bailey, 22 November 1817)

Sensations are self-authenticating. Once we try to convey them along with a glimpse of how they connect with all the other feelings, beliefs and memories that go to make up our selves, we immediately allow in – by the very workings of metaphorical language which we saw in chapter 4 – all the complementary (and antithetical) and parallel (and incongruent) experiences of the reader. The very means of making the connection is what makes the connection imprecise.

Does a poem ever reveal what the poet started out to say? As a critic I am unable to answer that question. When I look at the poets on my shelves from the mediaeval lyricists to Ted Hughes, from John Donne to Richard Wilbur, Spencer to Bernard O'Donoghue, I am faced with finished work: poems whose origins I cannot guess at, whose beginnings may, indeed, be as shrouded from the poets themselves as they are from me.

But, of course, there are one or two books that don't fall in this category; and they are the books that I have written myself. My experience as a writer may here throw some light on the critic's approach. Perhaps I should first say that my questioning of other poets has assured me that I am not a special case; that, by and large, my experience of the process of writing matches that of most poets and we can, for the purposes of this argument, ignore the value of the results of that process.

Because the process of writing is not one of autobiography but one of discovery, because one writes in order to find out what one thinks and how one sees, only very seldom does a poem seem to fulfil the plan or the framework one had, however vaguely, devised for it beforehand. Indeed, it seems to take an almost perverse pleasure in leaving its predestined tracks as soon as it possibly can.

A poem is a linguistic construct, and never more so than when it is actually being worked on and worked at. It can always, of course, be seen, even when finished, as a verbal device, but during the process of writing it feels like a *purely* verbal device. I'm afraid most writing about writing is liable to sound fairly pretentious because writing itself is chasing the inexpressible, and writing about that activity is the inexpressible at yet another remove, but the nearest I can get to it is to say that one is trying to find the tune. It is not that you have heard the tune and merely need to find the notation so that it can be heard by others, it is finding the words that will sing the tune that you have not yet truly heard yourself. When you start on a poem you do tend to think that you have heard the tune and only need to write down the notes, but that changes. You soon realize either that you had not heard a tune at all or that the tune you are chasing is a mere banality, or that everyone else has been whistling it for years. When this happens you either stop and go on to something else or you get a faint echo of the real tune that is there somewhere and begin to chase that one up.

That is why, although many poems begin with a word or a phrase that seems pregnant with all sorts of possibilities, by the time the poem is finished that word or that phrase will not appear in the poem at all. The 'brilliant' perception that started the whole thing off has finished up on the junk-heap.

This, of course, is to say that poetry is an art and not an accident. It is when you inspect a line and then change it to make it more musical (or less musical) or more clear, or faster-moving, when you find that there is only a silly or banal word which will provide the rhyme you need, and so you change the earlier lines, when you remove an alliteration that draws too much attention to itself, when you change an image in the light of a subsequent image – it is when you start doing this kind of work that you have to dig down into yourself and your understanding, your true feelings, your painful memories. And in doing that, you find yourself saying things that you did not know you knew. It has become an exploration, not a mere repetition of superficial knowledge.

Of course, if your idea of art is to slap down inchoate perceptions on a piece of paper, you will increase your output and cut down a great deal on the workload. You may even find yourself a following who think you're the best thing since pre-washed, vacuum-packed salad. But you will be missing a great deal, and so shall we.

Where, then, out of such purely verbal activity, does the 'saying' come in? If the art is not accidental, maybe the morality is?

That is to put it very strongly, but I think it is much closer to the truth than the view that a poem is a piece of morality or perceived truth that is then dressed up in beautiful words. C. S. Lewis puts it succinctly:

> what does not concern us deeply will not deeply interest our readers ... Let the pictures tell you their own moral. For the moral inherent in them will rise from whatever spiritual roots you have succeeded in striking during the whole course of your life ... the moral you *put in* is likely to be a platitude, or even a falsehood, skimmed from the surface of your consciousness.

> (Lewis, 'On Three Ways of Writing for Children', from Of Other Worlds; my italics)

You cannot become a different person in your writing from the person you are when you get out of bed in the morning. However you try to disguise it, the cast of your mind will give you away. This need not strike us with fear. The petty, spiteful, corrupt man will reveal himself as such, however much he tries to disguise it. The man of compassion and strength and humility will come through even when he is writing about a vase of flowers, a fishing expedition or a memory of his schooldays.

For even when a writer is not *putting in* attitudes, trying to *say* something, but rather making his assault on the intractability of language; even when the poem has derailed itself as soon as it's clear of the station, he has the choice – and it can be seen as a moral one – of admitting to what he has done and approving it, or throwing it away. You may not be able to publish the poems you want to, but you certainly don't have to publish the ones you don't want to.

It was only when I had been writing for a while that I fully understood and appreciated the truth behind the wit of Lewis Carroll's wordplay:

> 'Then you should say what you mean,' the March Hare went on.
> 'I do,' Alice hastily replied: 'at least – at least I mean what I say – that's the same thing, you know.'
> 'Not the same thing a bit!' said the Hatter.
>
> (Carroll, *Alice in Wonderland*)

The poet may have started off by trying to say what he meant and, having given that up, said something else. So long as he means what he says, it does not matter that his original attempt went awry. The Hatter is quite right; and I used to think Alice was right. The poet may have said something that neither he nor we expected, but, after he has surprised himself, he may look at the result and see if it is worth saying. So the dimension of truth, the moral dimension if you like to put it that way, is still there, though it has come about in a way we might not have expected.

Herbert, it seems to me, is the perfect example of a poet whose roots are fastened firmly in God and whose blossom of poetry is the product of that symbiosis. Godliness and wonder, I was going to say, tumble from Herbert, but that would not be true; they radiate from him, they step and dance and tread with perfect poise from his mind to ours, content and form, idea and language balanced, matched and, apparently, effortless. One feels of Herbert, more than any other poet, that the work and the man are one. I would compare him and contrast him with Hopkins. Without for a moment wishing to imply that Hopkins' beliefs were any less constant or profound than those of Herbert, he does sometimes appear to paste on to a poem a kind of Christian rider; the vision is not always quite as unified as Herbert's. This may be something to do with the double vocation of priest and poet, and maybe even more to do with the gap in his creativity that was forced on him by the discipline of the Jesuits – a feeling, perhaps, that when he did return to verse he must not fritter away his gifts on anything that was not overtly spiritual. The criticism does not apply to his very best work, which has a terrifying candour not to be found in any of his contemporaries; but it is difficult to escape the feeling that, however brilliantly a poem starts, with a lantern passing the window, a sky full of stars, a harvest-field rippling with corn, it is all going to remind him of Jesus and the last few lines are going to explain it all in a way that is both poetically unsatisfying and also predictable. For a moment he seems not to have trusted the God inside himself; and this is odd, considering the confidence that allowed him to continue writing his extraordinary poetry in the face of bewilderment and misunderstanding from Robert Bridges and others. It is not that one ever disbelieves Hopkins or questions his sincerity, it is rather that we are aware of the device, aware of the poem in a way that Herbert does not allow us to be; we may assent to Hopkins but we are changed by Herbert. Hopkins impresses, Herbert reveals. But then, when we come to poems such as 'Carrion comfort', 'No worst, there is none', 'To seem the stranger' and the other so-called 'Terrible' sonnets, the experience and its meaning are fused into one seamless poetic utterance, undiluted and unmediated.

It is easy to feel comfortable with Herbert and Hopkins; even if we don't actively enjoy their poetry, we feel safe in approving of it. They were both, whether Calvinist or Catholic, priests of their church, and their poems deal with the world in terms of their very specific beliefs. It is much harder to know where we are when we turn to a modern poet such as Philip Larkin. Since we know it was one of his favourite poems and we can, therefore, be sure that we are not choosing something uncharacteristic or something that he might have been tempted to disavow, let us look at his poem 'Absences':

> Rain patters on a sea that tilts and sighs.
> Fast-running floors, collapsing into hollows,
> Tower suddenly, spray-haired. Contrariwise,
> A wave drops like a wall: another follows,
> Wilting and scrambling, tirelessly at play
> Where there are no ships and no shallows.
>
> Above the sea, the yet more shoreless day,
> Riddled by wind, trails lit-up galleries:
> They shift to giant ribbing, sift away.
>
> Such attics cleared of me! Such absences!

Where do we start to look for what it tells us? The title is 'Absences' and the last word of the poem is 'absences', so we cannot be accused of being fanciful or reading too much into a short lyric when we suppose that the idea of absence is central. Whose absence? The poet's absence: he talks of attics cleared of 'me'.

So he is visualizing, in the first six lines, a seascape without any human dimension at all; it is a sea far from land, as is implicit in 'no ships and no shallows' – we are not on the coast, but miles from anywhere. It is, then, an entirely imagined scene, otherwise we would need at least one ship under the feet of the poet. But he is absent.

Is it a bleak scene? This is probably an important question, but the answer is liable to be subjective. Many people would see rain falling upon a limitless ocean as a pretty bleak picture, and the word 'sighs' tends to emphasize the miserable aspects of the picture rather than its wildness or naturalness. On the other hand, the sea is described very much in terms of one of those seaside attractions, a kind of house of fun where everything does what you don't expect. He talks of 'fast-running floors' which collapse and then rear up. 'Spray-haired' is an image more delightful than depressing, and he makes sure that we imagine the water 'tirelessly at play'. The sea is enjoying itself; despite or because there are no humans there?

We get a glimpse of emptiness and infinity in the next three lines; 'the yet more shoreless day'; and the 'giant ribbing' of the clouds does not last, but is allowed to 'sift away'. And then comes the clinching last line.

'Attics' and 'absences' are joined by the assonance of that first vowel, we are invited to connect them. Attics are generally the places where you find the most poignant and personal of a man's possessions; into the attic go the photograph albums, the old diaries, the teddy bears and beloved children's books and toys. But this world offers Larkin no such comforts. This attic is 'cleared' of him; nothing to cling on to, nothing to identify him. Even the rhyme-scheme is such that the last line is left unconnected to the rest of the poem. The second three lines are joined to the first six by the play/day/away rhyme, but the other rhyme evolves slowly in order to shed the last word: 'hollows' and 'follows' are perfect rhymes, but 'shallows' is a half-rhyme, beginning to move away, then 'galleries' takes us a step further away, and by the time we get to 'absences' we are completely unloosed from the rhyme of 'hollows' which started it all.

The only question left to answer now is whether the last line has become emotionally comprehensible; that is, whether it should be read as:

Such attics cleared of me! Such absences! (Hooray!)

or

Such attics cleared of me! Such absences! (Oh, hell!)

Or perhaps it is merely a statement of wonder – that nature has no need of man trying to find meanings in her illimitability.

Here we may see, quite clearly, that what the poet is trying to 'say' is not reducible to a message or an attitude, and whatever one would like to extract from the poem in terms of meaning must be seen in terms of *how* the poem works as an artefact.

Quotation can be misleading if the quotation is taken out of context. How many times have you heard that it was Keats who said:

> 'Beauty is truth, truth beauty,'

when in fact it was the Grecian urn speaking to Keats. How often do we attribute to Larkin this idea in the last line of his poem 'An Arundel Tomb':

> What will survive of us is love.

No wonder we find it surprising. Larkin is, in fact, more characteristically tentative than that, as can be seen when we add the previous line and a half:

>   to prove
> Our almost-instinct almost true:
> What will survive of us is love.

We must not look only at the words of a poem to find what a poet is communicating to us. A great deal of work is done by the form, and any poet who chucks away the multitudinous forms of English verse – those that exist and those that can be invented – is discarding a very important part of his armoury.

A poem gives us both an experience (the matter of the poem) and a sensibility (the manner of the poem), and the true work of art holds the two in tension. The verse of Shakespeare has never been criticized for diminishing the sometimes violent, disgusting realism of what it deals with. The anguish of Lear, the fearful visions of Macbeth and the dark, sordid imaginings of Leontes or Othello are not lessened but heightened by the superb flexibility of the verse in which they are written. What is in effect a negative experience is being held by a positive sensibility; one which can place the experience, see beyond it, contain it. Art is not life. Whatever light the one sheds on the other, they are not identical, and that is why I reject Damien Hirst's famous sheep in formaldehyde as well as chaotic and unfocused free verse as being lower than art. Art demands the framework of a sensibility, it does not just shove things beneath your nose and leave you to make of it what you can. That's what life does. Art contains chaos: it presents a framework for order and achievement precisely so that it may let us see clearly the disorder with which it deals.

Art, whether it is verbal or visual, must contain the means by which it may be understood. A piece of art that *has* to be explained, that needs a key apart from the work itself, is not art, it is code. I have avoided the truism that art is communication, partly because it is a truism and partly because it is a great deal more than simply communication, and in that 'great deal more' the really interesting things are to be found. But art is at *least* communication, whereas accidents can communicate nothing more than that such things happen.

And yet art, while it needs to be self-explanatory, is not likely to be easily explicable. It communicates on all sorts of different levels at the same time. A character talking about what he believes (or a narrator telling us the same thing) is the very simplest level of meaning. What a character does is another level of meaning. Yet another can be found in what other characters say or think about him, and in the various things that happen to him; surprises, accidents, coincidences, even the weather can contain metaphors and symbols which have a bearing on the affectiveness and effectiveness of a story.

Browning, that novelist who never wrote a novel, has baffled many readers by his portrayal of 'Mr Sludge the Medium', a poem which hardly any readers seem to be able to approach without prejudice. Mr Sludge may appear to us as a vulgar charlatan, a fake and a cheat. But that does not mean that he is *merely* a vulgar charlatan. What the poem is doing is exploring the borderland between truth and falsehood, honesty and trickery, and what Mr Sludge is telling us is that the boundaries are not as well-defined or as easily recognized as we might think. Because he has committed a fraud, we must not assume that all of his calling are fraudsters; just because he has faked the spiritual world does not mean that the idea of a spiritual world is a fake, any more than that an example of immorality should lead us to believe that there is no such thing as morality. Just the opposite is the case.

Browning is not much read and not much liked these days, and I wonder if it is because we cannot distinguish between confusion and challenge: we want false blacks and whites, not truthful greys. For what Browning does again and again, not just in 'Mr Sludge the Medium,' is to put profound and resonant truths into the mouths of characters we despise. We find it comfortable to believe that good people say good things and bad people say bad things, but this is simplistic nonsense. Browning will have none of it, and nor should we. Truth is truth whether it come from a beautiful source or a grotesque one. That, though obliquely transmitted, is one of Browning's themes, and, I hope, will be remembered as one of the themes of this book.

We should remember in all humility that it was of an outsider, an oppressor of his people, an unbeliever from a nation that was to be technically responsible for his death, that Jesus said:

> I say unto you, I have not found so great faith, no, not in Israel.
>
> (Luke 7.9)

8

*Poetry makes nothing happen**

———◦⌐———

When you read that sentence from Auden which is used as this chapter's title, did your heart sink or sing? Did it delight you to think that poetry could not be subservient to any particular creed, philosophy or political bias? Or did you think: 'So much the worse for poetry'? The quotation does not, of course, apply only to poetry. There is a story about a writer who sat in a courtroom and, at the end of the morning's session was heard to remark, almost certainly with a sigh, 'When that judge sentences some poor devil to go to prison for five years, he goes. But when I publish a book nothing happens!' The immediate sympathy that such a remark arouses leads to two further questions: the first is, should anything happen in a practical sense, as the result of publishing a piece of fiction or poetry? The second is, does it? Were Auden and our anonymous writer misled when they thought nothing happened?

When I put this question to Ted Hughes his response was:

I think one of the strongest ingredients in the collapse of the Soviet system was the poetry written in Eastern Europe and in Russia; poetry that kept alive, focused, found the attitudes, the basic standing-point that gave definition to the feeling that finally brought them

*W. H. Auden: 'In Memory of W. B. Yeats II'

122

down. And I think that was, yes, poetry doing its real job.

(Hughes, interview with the author)

That is clear enough. What is not clear is whether the poets were writing a kind of purposive poetry, one that was consciously aimed at bringing about such a result. Almost certainly some were; but Hughes seems tacitly to be admitting that it was not a case of simple cause and effect. The poetry, he says, kept alive a standpoint that defined a feeling that brought the collapse, and that, it seems to me, is precisely right. The poetry was an iteration of personal truth and integrity, of living, vital feelings; not propaganda, but a standard to which the poet must bear witness even when it seems pointless and self-defeating. One of the best examples is the poetry of Irina Ratushinskaya, mostly written in the most horrific prison conditions, at great personal risk and under the torture of not knowing what had happened to her husband and family. Her story, and that of thousands of others, is so shocking and so moving that it goes a long way to making us feel that poetry is nothing if it does not scream against political oppression and inhumanity. The world must be changed and, against that fact, it feels merely feeble sometimes to be concerned with beauty or landscape or love or the intellect. There are, surely, more important things in life than this.

But let us not forget that probably exactly the same thoughts kept Irina Ratushinskaya strong and sane. Lonely and hopeless in her icy prison, she could be sustained by the thought that 'There are more important things in life than this.' To put it another way, if poetry is always about desolation, to what may the desolate turn for strength? If our poetry rails all the time against ugliness, where may our minds go to find beauty? Yes, this side of Eden and this side of heaven, the world will always need changing, but are the arts necessarily the best way to effect that change?

It depends how and where you see that change taking place. In this respect the arts and Christianity meet again on common ground. What Christianity offers is the same as that which Seamus Heaney sees poetry offering: a redress, a restoration of balance, salt, light, call it what you will, but it does it as it were by stealth rather than by proclamation, by being rather than by asserting. For balance can only be achieved once everything is in the scales; leave something out and you haven't got balance at all, only some kind of temporary equivalence which can be destroyed by adding another aspect of the truth.

This is what the propagandist refuses to see. He has a vision, but it is a tunnel vision; it may be a good vision, but it lacks truth in proportion as it lacks inclusiveness. Every exclusive truth given clarity and voice is a denial or at least an ignoring of other truths which may be considered of equal importance. You cannot set up a theory which will hold water by wilfully ignoring any evidence that conflicts with it.

The propagandist's aim is to win the argument. The poet's aim, and the Christian's aim, is to tell the truth and, indeed, to shame the devil. Any lies, distortions and over-simplifications will do for the propagandist because the end justifies the means. None will be acceptable to the poet or the honest Christian. You cannot make the world right by being wrong. You cannot achieve purity by the constant application of more and more impurities.

Christ himself is the perfect example of balance, and it is precisely this that the church loses when it picks out aspects of his teaching and promotes them as being central. The truth is that *Christ* is central, and if we give any of his teachings the place that he himself should occupy we run the risk of upsetting the balance.

Let us make another diagram. Put Christ in the centre and then circle him with all that he taught. That is the true picture. Now take 'justice' or 'healing' or 'power over death', put that in the middle and put Christ himself where that came from, on the circumference, and you have the perfect recipe for well-intentioned imbalance, distortion and, possibly, fanaticism. Once we had the Inquisition, now we have a kind of weak-kneed triumphalism. Both are deadly and both are the result of moving Christ from the centre and replacing him with whatever suits us. But Christianity wasn't ever meant to suit us, it was meant to restore our balance.

When religion becomes propaganda it ceases to work; when poetry becomes propaganda the same thing happens. Simplification is not generally a mode of any work of art, and over-simplification never is. One might allow children's literature to be less stringent than that, but in the best children's books we don't find the kind of black-and-white oppositions that we might feel ourselves willing to accept. In Joan Aiken's books about Dido Twite, Dido's father is a feeble-willed, avaricious and wicked man who will not stop at sacrificing his daughter if it brings him advancement; and, at the same time, he is a musician and composer of genius who can speak through his music with the accents of angels. Browning would have enjoyed such a creation, and it is one of the things that brings real depth and honesty to a story which could so easily have become tidily moral. Instead, it is movingly honest.

What I have been at pains to point out as being the true virtues of literature, the very things that make it work – wholeness of perception, truth to human nature and irreducibility to mere message – are the very things that propaganda must eschew if it is to be effective. Propaganda depends on avoiding certain issues and questions in order to hammer home its solutions. Literature depends on opening up as many questions and feelings and ideas as possible in order to show that all solutions are partial, all are fraught with difficulties. Propaganda forms prejudices, literature is out to destroy them.

That is not to say that poetry can never be practical, but it will never be practical in the way that politics is. Governments can shape, require, legislate and force; poetry cannot – but it can convince, and that is its true power. In a sense a party manifesto is not unlike a poem. It is a dream, a 'what if?', a future possibility to counterbalance the present, a way of making sense of our present existence. But the poet's job ends when he has written the poem; the government has to find ways of making that dream possible. The poet is judged by the truth and beauty of his dream, the government by its practical success or failure. But then, the government can always shift the blame: the poet must take full responsibility. The government may find ways to bribe or pacify us or help us forget our moral concerns. The poet can do none of this: he stands or falls by the poor, naked truth.

So our writer in the courtroom, envying the power of the judge, need not feel too downhearted. The main difference between them is that the judge's power is public and its effectiveness may be seen by all. The power of literature is private, unseen except by him who reads and feels. Temporal power speaks to the world, or at least to the mob; literary power speaks to the individual spirit. The judge can make sure that the man is convicted, but the writer can make sure he is convinced. A book of poems may do more to change a man's heart and mind than any number of public and political pronouncements; and if art speaks quietly to the individual rather than in clichés to the committee ('God so loved the world', goes the quotation, 'that he did not send a committee'), then it must not, it dare not, be a mouthpiece for one single point of view.

What Christianity has claimed for so long is true of art as well: it can change societies and nations, but it can only do so by changing the individual. Masses may be swayed but not changed. When individuals begin to change, then the change affects society and society changes as well; but no dictum, no law, no instruction, however well-intentioned, can change society from the outside.

A poem, a play, a novel can have an immense influence on an individual; it can be life-changing, but not in the magical way, the immediate way, the superficial way that a win on the lottery might change him. Literature moves more slowly and more surely than that. It awakes and informs parts of the imagination that have lain dormant, it opens possibilities and enlarges visions; it changes priorities. And when priorities change lives begin to be lived very differently. A does not suddenly change to Q, but it steps to B and then to C, and then the hitherto unimaginable D comes into sight, and so it goes on.

But this is not a process that can be triggered by propaganda. It takes more delicacy and suggestiveness than the blunt certainties that are offered by the blinkered vision of the propagandist. Again, Keats can sum it up for us:

We hate poetry that has a palpable design upon us.
(Keats, letter to Reynolds, 3 February 1818)

And we hate it because it closes the world down to certainties instead of opening it up to the range and scope of existence where we may discover our own certainties. This can even be seen in the world of the interpretative arts. When a director finds in a Shakspeare play some single theme or a connection that can be made with contemporary concerns and then proceeds to costume, design and direct the play in order to highlight that single aspect, to illustrate his *idea*, the play loses much of its significance; Shakespeare is not saying this or that, and to focus the production so that he seems to be is untrue to the richness and ambiguity of the text. When we see the play we might find it quite a powerful theatrical experience, but that experience has been had at the expense of the one Shakespeare unmeddled-with could have given us. When we see it we meet only the mind of the director, which is fine so long as the mind of the director is as profound and creative as the mind of Shakespeare; but how many of them are? What was true for all time has been reduced to special pleading, what was an exploration has become an expression; the concept has destroyed as much as it has revealed. This is not propaganda, as such, but in its selectivity of approach and in the various denials and blurrings that must be accommodated, it works in a very similar way to propaganda.

From what I have said so far, it may seem that I have

little sympathy with any political, religious or social movement that is trying to change and improve the world and
am standing up for a kind of vague, uncommitted eclecti-
cism. On the contrary, I can see as clearly as anyone else
that the world is cruel and cynical, selfish and thoughtlessly
prodigal – perhaps not a great deal more than at any time
in the past, but with a new and frightening capability for
destructiveness and perhaps a terminal fouling of its own
nest – but whatever determination I may have to do something about it will be expressed in action or journalism, not
in literature. I would rather save forests than destroy them
in order to print bad poems about why we should save
forests.

I think I can imagine the various sorts of pressure that
must have been put on the Irish poets with an international
voice such as Michael Longley and Seamus Heaney to take
a stand about the troubles in Ireland; to denounce and to
protest. Bravely, they have both demurred, preferring what
Heaney called images 'appropriate to our predicament'
which have informed poems of pained but wise integrity: a
counterbalance, a still, small voice amid the slogan-shouting
and the clamour. This, too, is poetry doing its real job.

All this is not to say that writers are not people; they
must cook and get their children to school and clean out
the fire and wash their hair like the rest of the world. And,
like the rest of the world, they may vote Labour or Liberal
or Conservative, be vegetarian or carnivore, agree or disagree with the penal system and believe or disbelieve in
God. But what makes them good citizens is quite different
from what makes them good writers. We talk about the
artistic *temperament*, and in doing so we speak, perhaps,
more truly than we notice, for (unless we are misusing
the expression to mean selfish and difficult behaviour) we
are acknowledging that the mind of the true artist is one
that is tempered: where all the elements are mixed and
proportioned and balanced. Such a temperament is a long
way from that of the soldier, the politician and the single-
issue fanatic. This, incidentally, may explain why so many

painters, writers, composers, artists of all kind are to be seen at rallies and protests and political (with a large or small 'p') meetings: they are displaying a part of their make-up which cannot be given voice in their work or, since their occupations are solitary ones, in their workplace. They will also be to the forefront since, human nature being what it is, and any kind of fame being attractive, they will have been pushed there. Many will enjoy that; many will not.

But does this mean that the writer cannot have a vision, a faith, even a point of view? Must he always merely describe? Are only secular and natural values to be taken seriously? The answer to all these questions is no, as may be confirmed by a glance at any of the poetry written over the last five hundred years. One may speak, believe, suggest and conclude without resort to propaganda.

I have been seeking examples of bad, propagandistic poetry to support my point, but it is even better supported by the fact that I cannot find any. In other words, it has not found its way into the collections and the anthologies, simply because it was not considered worthwhile keeping. I have implied that if it is art at all it is substandard art, and that seems to have been borne out by the filtering process of history. There are, of course, some patriotic verses and jingoistic pieces by writers such as Newbolt, Kipling, Noyes and many others, and some of these lean very strongly towards propaganda in a very general sense. Sometimes that element is small enough to be subsumed within the greater sensibility of the whole, sometimes it tastes so strong that it overwhelms the rest of the poem and mars it irreparably. Propaganda soon passes its sell-by date.

At precisely what point any proselytizing element becomes too much for the poem to bear while still remaining a poem rather than becoming a tract or a sermon, is impossible to establish and it will nearly always be subject to taste and opinion. We must look hard at all the elements in the poem and remind ourselves that the goodness of a piece of writing is not solely to be judged on whether its content is acceptable to us, nor is it to be considered bad because it presents a point of view which is not our own.

We are now on the verge of having to make a distinction which is far from easy but which probably has to be made: the distinction between art and craft. It has often been said that one may be an artist without being a propagandist but that it is impossible to be a propagandist without being at least competent as an artist. I would say that the second time that word 'artist' appears is where the error creeps in. One does not need to be an artist; only a craftsman.

Art and craft overlap. If they did not it would be much easier to distinguish between them, but they do. There is craft, there is technique involved in a work of art, but there is more – and in craft there is nothing more. I have already called art an exploration, and that implies that, whatever means are employed, the end is never predictable. In craft, the finished product is planned and visualized before the process of making it even starts. In a sense you cannot judge the success of a piece of art, because there are no criteria against which it can be measured; but a work of craft will be successful if it achieves the end it set out to achieve.

One could, for instance, say a lot of useful and intelligent things about *Macbeth,* but to call it a successful play would not be one of them. The term is meaningless when applied to art. A table can be successful, when it is the right height and width, when it doesn't wobble, when the surface is flat and level; anything that has a preordained purpose can be successful. But a work of art, whether it is a symphony, a painting or a poem, is simply what it is – the form finally taken by certain emotional and intellectual impulses: self-consistent, unforeseen and, in the end, inexplicable. Of course, on the level of sheer craftmanship it should not wobble – or whatever the dramatic equivalent of an unsuccessful table does – and it must be felt as being the right size for its shape and energy, and so on. But these judgements will necessarily have been made after the event: they could not have been foreseen, since there was no blueprint for the work and it was more than simply will and skill.

Because I have (just) sufficient knowledge, I could write a short movement for violin and piano on the level of a kind of craftmanship; it would not puzzle any musician I gave it to and would not disobey the laws of harmony. It might even have a certain naive charm, who knows? But if you were to compare it with anything Mozart wrote even before he was a teenager, you would very soon see the difference between craft and art: my plodding and predictable banalities, stiff and limited: his sheer imaginative and creative power.

The craftsman assembles his materials and whatever tools he needs before he starts work; nothing else is necessary apart from the time to complete the task, and that, too, can be predicted within a little. But the poor writer cannot even prepare his materials. Tools, yes: he can provide himself with pen and paper, but where *is* his material? It is not sufficient to say 'in the dictionary', because it doesn't work like that. He doesn't empty out a dozen of 'the', three of 'love', two of ''twas', a 'hope', a 'beauty', a 'duty' and an assortment of conjunctions and then try to fit together a poem out of this given material. The poem starts much earlier than in the choice of the verbal matter. Quite where, nobody has yet been able to pin down, and poets can't help because they don't know either, and it may seen to be tempting fate if they ask. Besides, one man's methods and habits may differ completely from another's even if they are consistent. And as to time, any poet will tell you that it may take twenty minutes to write an eight-line poem; it may take twenty months.

This is not the place to attempt a definition of art, even supposing I thought I could be successful where so many others have failed. But, in contrast to craft, let us recall the idea of exploration and the man who writes or paints in order to discover his ideas and feelings to himself. Let us recall the power of the imagination which, like the Spirit, 'bloweth where it listeth'; let us think of an organic vision of great power, captured sufficiently to be able to communicate something of that power, though never completely; something that transcends its parts by being a great deal more, even though the whole of literary, musical and artistic criticism has been unable to tell us unequivocally where and how that 'more' is to be found.

No, it is not art but craft that produces propaganda. The writer knows what his goal is – to convince a certain sort of person that a certain sort of action is expedient – and he bends his skills to that end. If the writer in question is an artist whose real talents are being prostituted and exploited (as opposed to someone who can 'knock out a few lines from time to time'), then the writing may, unbidden, begin to slip further and further towards true art. The result will probably be ineffective as propaganda because it is too complex and interesting, and unacceptable as art because it is too full of message to have any lasting imaginative impact.

Unerring lines and distinctions cannot be drawn in literature: poetry and prose, art and craft, metaphor and truth either overlap or meet at a point where one is indistinguishable from another. I have tried to state the argument against propaganda clearly and nakedly, but it's never as clear cut when we come up against it, particularly in works of the past. In the novel, especially, since it is such a baggy and discursive form, and nowhere more so than in its nineteenth-century heyday, elements of what might be called impurity may be smuggled in without too much upset. A fine writer can turn all sorts of unlikely things into art. But what happens more often than not is that in reading literature of the past we do not notice the propaganda element because, first, it has been so well assimilated into the whole; and, second, because whatever was being urged has, by now, become a dead issue. The nearer we get to the present the more alive the issues will be and the more conscious of them we will be. Thus, a poem written in 1940 urging young men to join the army and go and fight will be irrevocably linked in the minds of anybody of forty or over with the specific issues of the Second World War. A poem urging just the same thing but written in the sixteenth century is much more likely to be seen as a general attitude, a philosophical position, and, even if it is found wanting, to be judged as art first and propaganda second, if at all.

The relative importance and salience of such elements will depend too upon the scale of the work in question. If the novel is – metaphorically speaking – a biplane, there will be some sorts of freight it won't be able to carry. But if it is a jumbo jet, it will be capable of much more before it becomes overloaded.

Dickens and Bunyan provide us with very good examples of works which are still read and loved, which are unmistakably works of art, and yet which are just as unmistakably works of propaganda bent on changing the world in the case of Dickens and opening the spiritual eyes of man in the case of Bunyan. Dickens, of course, never conceived his works as anything like pure propaganda, it was one of the themes he could and would tackle, and even though Bunyan almost certainly did have a distinct and particular moral purpose in *The Pilgrim's Progress*, he has cast it in the form of a parable and of a dream so that it is at least two steps away from rhetoric and makes its points obliquely. Most importantly, there is both wit and acute observation at the centre of it, and the abstractions which he personifies speak with the accents of real flesh-and-blood Bedfordshire people. Truth to his material rather than to some abstract aim is what has turned it into art.

It is difficult to tell what effect it has had, for such effects are not measurable. With Dickens it is somewhat easier. He

did really destroy some of the wrongs he hated and bring about some of the reforms he desired. Dickens did help pull down the debtors' prisons ... Dickens did drive Squeers out of his Yorkshire den ... Dickens did leave his mark on parochialism, on nursing, on funerals, on public executions, on workhouses, on the

Court of Chancery. These things were altered; they are different. It may be that such reforms are not adequate remedies; that is another question altogether. The next sociologists may think these old Radical reforms quite narrow or accidental. But such as they were, the old Radicals got them done; and the new sociologists cannot get anything done at all.

(G. K. Chesterton, *Dickens*, ch. 11)

Occasionally Dickens can be said to over-emphasize, to protest too much and risk spoiling the ship by applying just too much tar, but he is already at a distance where the oppressions he describes can be seen as part of his world rather than as something we feel genuine moral outrage in confronting. The poverty he describes may still have power to move us to action, for that, sadly, is still with us; but Victorian funerals, workhouses and executions are already part of a kind of mythology; and, besides, his characters are so huge, so energetic, so grotesque, so singular and substantial that the world they move in must be similarly extreme. We don't really care that his world was, in fact, true, because it is entirely appropriate. Art, assisted by time, has subsumed propaganda. Bunyan, on the other hand, because he is dealing with eternal matters – not only eternity itself but the unchanging material of the human heart – is much more uncomfortably close to home. Even if we read him as art we can't entirely escape the frisson of what lurks behind the art. How far and in what ways literature and religious beliefs inform each other will be the subject of the next chapter.

9

It is requir'd you do awake your faith *

———

Doctor Johnson, writing about Gray's 'Elegy written in a Country Churchyard', gave it praise for the following reason:

> [It] abounds with images which find a mirror in every mind and with sentiments to which every bosom returns an echo.
>
> (Johnson, 'Thomas Gray', *Lives of the English Poets*)

It would be a dull sort of literature that did nothing but confirm, repeat and present to us our own opinions, our own ideas and our own prejudices; but Johnson is here putting his finger on a very important truth about the way we read and understand literature. Anything that we read we compare, consciously or unconsciously, with our own knowledge, feelings and beliefs – those components of what I have called our world-view, that scarcely noticed but continuous underlying pressure of thought that we can never deny and that is a matrix against which all our perceptions are tested.

Let us take the simplest case possible. When a poet says 'tree' we are not lost for a reference point. It would take a psychologist to explain exactly what happens in the brain

* Shakespeare: *The Winter's Tale* act 5, scene 3

when a word is recognized and attached to a mental image, but, for the moment we can agree that, if we have all seen plenty of trees, something 'tree-y' and sufficient will be entertained by our imaginations. If the poet says 'apple tree' or 'beech tree' or 'holly tree', we can focus and refine our vision appropriately. Along with our mental vision of the tree will come various associations both general and personal, for even an intensely visual image is never merely visual: it will be mixed up with scents, particularly, with texture and, where appropriate, with taste and sound.

The resultant image will in many cases be emotionally neutral – a simple recognition. But there will be some cases where a very vivid and even unpredictable association is made if the object imagined has had an important role in the reader's life. I might, for instance, include a holly tree in a poem for its associations with Christmas, early darkness, firelight, winter morning walks; for the brightness of its berries in contrast with the monochrome frosts or fogs of late November. Because these associations are not entirely personal, because the context will help to explain my vision and because, even if hitherto unnoticed, the associations make sense, the image is likely to work.

But what if my reader's association with holly trees has been one of terror or pain? What if the gloomy holly trees that surrounded his house and scraped at his windows on stormy nights had been a trouble to his dreams? What if he had been thrown into a holly bush time after time during his schooldays as a punishment for infringing some code of schoolboy behaviour or dropping an easy catch at cricket? Then his feelings about holly trees would not be easily separable from his emotional memories of fear and humiliation. Nothing, however objective it may look on paper, comes without its associations. As Christopher Fry puts it:

A spade is never so merely a spade as the word
Spade would imply.

(Fry, *Venus Observed*, act 2, scene 1)

This is all quite straightforward and, indeed, obvious. But it need not be a barrier to understanding or appreciation unless the memory is disturbing to the point of obsession or trauma. When a good reader meets a text, what actually happens is that, albeit unconsciously, personal associations are set aside and the reader surrenders to what the writer is doing. This is what Coleridge called, in a phrase that has now become almost a cliché, the willing suspension of disbelief.

Because the expression has become so worn and familiar, it is worth taking a moment to examine exactly what it means; and I think it means more than we usually allow.

At its simplest, it can be taken as a description of the thought-processes of the theatregoer as he settles into his seat; something along the lines of: 'Although I know that this play has been written and rehearsed in advance and that nothing that is going to happen in the next two and a quarter hours is real, I shall make myself forget this and I shall surrender to the make-believe. I will prevent myself remembering that Ophelia is only my dentist's receptionist and that six years ago I helped Hamlet through his A-level Sociology. I will see stage blood as real blood, faked death as real death and a rather badly painted piece of canvas as the wild seas below Elsinore.'

But the suspension of disbelief, the allowing of a fiction, whether it be a book, a play or a poem, to have its proper effect, goes deeper than this. We must also suspend (suspend, not obliterate) our prejudices, convictions and our most sincerely held opinions in order that the work may speak. This may sound like a renunciation of responsibility and integrity, but it isn't; the same thing happens when we are arguing with a friend; at least, it happens if we are genuinely arguing and not merely taking up a position of intractable obstinacy. We listen carefully, we don't assume the conclusion, we do not interrupt; in fact we suspend our judgement until we have heard the evidence, until the case under consideration has been put. Only in this way can any mental or spiritual development take place.

It seems that, in essence, we have only three choices: we

can accept nothing that anybody says or writes unless it corresponds minutely and unwaveringly to our own pre-conceptions, or we can accept everything that we read quite uncritically, or we can read with an open mind and then concede, demur, admit and argue and discover that we are being refined and that our sympathies and understanding are being enlarged by the process. This is the way literature must be read.

The suspension of disbelief is not only a willingness to go along with the writer and take our orders from the text, it is also, as we have seen, a kind of deliberate denial as well. Our playgoer has to deny the associations of the dental surgery when he watches Ophelia; and, as far as possible, the man who is terrified of holly trees must forget, overcome, that terror while he is reading, and allow himself to be swayed by the writer's vision of holly trees. If he can do that, he may even find the process healing.

Perhaps the willing suspension of disbelief is most easily imagined as a kind of dressing-up. It may start as little more than a pretence, but that changes. Put on a cloak, and you will soon find yourself standing straighter, walking more gracefully; the slouch and the shamble soon disappear. This kind of pretence, according to C. S. Lewis, is at the heart of our activity as Christians, and with the approval of God. While Lewis admits that there are bad pretences, he finds scriptural justification for good and enlarging ones. The Lord's Prayer, he reminds us, begins with the words 'Our Father':

> Do you now see what those words mean? They mean quite frankly, that you are putting yourself in the place of a son of God. To put it bluntly, you are *dressing up as Christ.* If you like, you are pretending. Because, of course ... you are not a being like The Son of God, whose will and interests are at one with those of the Father ... So that, in a way, this dressing up as Christ is a piece of outrageous cheek. But the odd thing is that He has ordered us to do it.
>
> (Lewis, *Mere Christianity*, Bk 4, ch. 7, 'Let's Pretend')

In just this way we, as readers, play 'Let's Pretend' when we meet a text. We suspend our disbelief in what we see or read and, just as importantly, we suspend our true beliefs – those beliefs we hold in the non-fictional world – in order properly to appreciate what the author is striving for. So, even if we are teetotallers, we must allow Falstaff to enjoy his bottle of sack; even if we cannot find it in ourselves to believe in life on other planets, we must leave that aside if we are to discover the truths in *The Day of the Triffids*. Fully to understand *Henry V* we must first remove any republican spectacles; *Moby-Dick* is best read after we have taken off our 'Save the Whale' badges.

But what happens when we come to writers who explore aspects of the Christian faith in their work? What happens when we come upon the opposite: writers who by their narratives, their images, the selectivity with which they describe or portray the world, implicitly deny any kind of Christian truth? Can we, should we suspend belief and disbelief in these instances? After all, it is one thing to take up a stance on the morality of whaling or the rights and wrongs of the monarchy versus the republic, it is rather a different thing to offer a whole range of presuppositions about the way the world is governed, man's relationship to the universe and the very source of morality and authority which are ultimately opposed to those of the reader. How can reader and writer find any common ground?

It is not a sufficient answer to reply, 'They can't', because even one example of the opposite case will be enough to refute such an answer, and I can supply several. I have seen a militant and intelligent atheist moved to tears by George Herbert's poem 'Prayer'; and scores of people with no Christian belief worth speaking of are lovers of Hopkins, Donne, Dante, Milton, Vaughan and Traherne.

As an example of the opposite position – Christians singularly moved by and attracted to works that continually ignore or deny the most basic tenets of the Christian faith – I can offer myself and my deep love of Thomas Hardy. In these cases it is patently obvious that the philosophy underpinning the works does not revolt or alienate the reader. Why not?

There are two answers that may tempt us, so let us consider them and reject them straightaway.

The first is that any mentions of Christ or God or the Holy Spirit are not really anything to do with belief but are vague references put in for form's sake and in order to give a specious air of authority, even timelessness, to the writer's own feelings. In other words, we should read these references and treat them rather as we might treat references to Zeus, Aphrodite, Mars, Apollo or 'rosy-fingered Dawn rising from Tithonus' bed' in the old classical authors; or as we might read invocations to the Muse, to the Spirit of Poesy, and so forth. They are there simply because it is the proper way to do these things, a kind of poetic etiquette. At best they are merely nods in the direction of the numinous which are supposed to add a kind of instant depth to the poet's perceptions.

This will not do. Partly because it is doubtful whether even for Homer or Sophocles, Ovid or Virgil, the gods had anything like the importance or the status that the Trinity has for the Christian. They were never much more than embodied superstitions. A sacrifice to the gods was much more like crossing your fingers or touching wood than it was like true worship. So, while we may read the classical authors in this way – they make the right noises, they toe the poetic party-line – we cannot read Bunyan in this way, or Hopkins or Donne, or any Christian writer. Their God is not a fiction to add verisimilitude; their faith is not a toy or a rhetorical tool or an optional extra, it is the ground of their being and very often the mode of their perception.

I have, admittedly, criticized Hopkins for his occasional habit of tacking on his Christian conclusion, but this is a literary not a doctrinal criticism; by which I mean that, although I may personally agree with his conclusion and assent to his world-view, his fervent belief that God is gloriously perceptible in the natural world whether it be in the bend of an ash branch or the spread of the stars, I don't think he has made of the poem a convincing whole. From reading his letters and his life we can be absolutely certain that there was nothing optional or tacked on about his belief in God, it was essential; my criticism is that he has not managed to persuade the reader that it is essential. Such poems do allow the reader to dismiss God, as we now dismiss Apollo and Phaeton and Atropos, as an orthodox piety. But let the reader take 'I Wake and Feel the Fell of Dark', 'Carrion Comfort' and the other sonnets in that fearful set, and he will not honestly be able to ascribe the emotions he meets to a touch of indigestion, a fit of the blues or a mere nod in the direction of deity. These are serious and memorable poems, all the more so for the seamless matching of form to content.

This brings us to the second tempting answer.

The content of a poem that is contrary to the beliefs of the reader (so this answer goes) somehow gets dismissed. What the reader responds to is the art, the music, the inter-play of images, the rhyme-scheme, the satisfaction of the formal control. *What* is says does not matter: what is important is how it says it.

This will not do either. Of course these are all immensely important aspects of the way poetry works, and neither poet nor reader may neglect them, but they are not the be-all and end-all. They are not the reason for poetry, nor are they in themselves poetry.

Poets write about things that are important to them; novelists, poets and dramatists explore ideas, not just images and sounds. In literature, sensual and aesthetic appreciation have to go hand in hand with some kind of illumination or evaluation of experience, otherwise you get nothing more than an abstract noise, and among all the attempted definitions of poetry there have been, I have yet to come across that one.

Music, on the other hand, *is* an abstract noise: it is meant to be. And because music is pattern and texture, purely aesthetic appreciation is possible. We delight in comformity and non-comformity, in the shift from discord to concord, in the fulfilling or dashing of our expectations. It is perhaps useless to complain that many people feel the need to ascribe some sort of meaning to that pattern, that noise: it is 'heroic' or 'pessimistic' or 'life-affirming'; but it must be conceded that such feelings are purely subjective (see Hindemith's comments in chapter 6) in a way that poetry must not be. Indeed, poetry cannot be entirely subjective in that way so long as the writer uses words that appear in our dictionaries and forms that seem to be appropriate and sufficient. How can any form be appropriate or otherwise if there is no substance, no content, for it to give form to?

We seem to be left with our problem. How can we respond to literature which is founded upon beliefs which we find abhorrent?

True, there are some who cannot, but they tend to be the single-issue fanatics who probably don't waste their valuable campaigning time in reading anything except books written by those who will echo and pander to their prejudices. But this will not be literature in the sense that we have been talking of literature.

The true answer is, I believe, to do with the imagination and its workings. When we pick up a play or a poem or a novel, we do so with a very different attitude from the one we adopt – consciously or subconsciously – when we pick up a book which purports to teach us something – a book on philosophy or religion, on cookery or gardening or air strategy in the Second World War. There, the truths are of a different order from the truths that fiction gives us. It is in some ways a pity that we have to use the same word for both of them, but it should not cause us too much difficulty. We have already noticed, in chapter 2, the different truths expressed by the three statements: 'The temperature is minus three degrees centigrade,' 'It is bitterly cold outside,' and 'Tonight the wind gnaws/ with teeth of glass.' Paradoxically, the truths which matter most to us are the unprovable ones: I am loved by you, I have toothache, I remember. How easily these are proved on our pulses, and how difficult they are to explain or analyse. These are the truths that literature tries to deal with. This is what we go to literature for: an illumination of what it means to be human.

But if we look for that kind of illumination we must also be prepared to find the immense variety of what can be illumined, and from what unusual angles the light that illuminates may fall.

So the first thing we do preparatory to accepting a fictional truth is tell ourselves that it is a fictional truth; that the framework of belief or unbelief is one which affects the characters in the book and has power over the reader only in as much as he allows it to. A thunderstorm in a book is not going to remove the tiles from your roof; nor is an evil thought or action going to stain your immortal soul. You may read about an experience undergone by a character in a novel that chimes uncannily with your own, and you may pause to wonder whether his interpretation of it, his reaction to it, was more honest, more full of integrity, perhaps, than your own; and in that sense it will have changed you, made you open to something you had not considered before. But then, in the world of reality you still have to make a decision based on your own beliefs and world-view as to whether you are going to take the matter any further. You still have your free will; you still have to make decisions based on your beliefs, your character, your circumstances, not on some fictional character's situation. You have been extended in your sympathies, not coerced. We have already compared reading a book with the games that children play. Here is G. K. Chesterton on the subject:

> the real child does not confuse fact and fiction. He simply likes fiction. He acts it, because he cannot as yet write it or even read it; but he never allows his moral sanity to be clouded by it. To him no two things could possibly be more totally contrary than playing at robbers and stealing sweets.
>
> (Chesterton, *Autobiography*, ch. 2, 'The Man with the Golden Key')

Beliefs, even when they are the very life-blood of the work as in Milton or Hopkins, matter much less than we might think, in terms of being either a barrier or a magnet for the reader. Why? Because what has happened, once the work has come into being, is that on the foundations of a profound belief has been reared an edifice of the imagination, not one of theology or propaganda or nihilism, but of the imagination. And it is this, through all the various resources of language and imagery, of surprise and repetition, of character and landscape, of chiming with our own memories here, revealing the hitherto unrecognized there, that draws us into an artistic experience which, if it is well and fairly done, transcends the beliefs and may even become – through that imaginative element – the means by which the beliefs may be countenanced and understood as possible.

It is impossible to draw any definite lines, but I dare say that even a work as packed with religious significance as *Paradise Lost* is more than 80 per cent intelligible human experience and less than 20 per cent Christian doctrine. Christians who have been brought up on C. S. Lewis and read his stories to their own children may find it difficult to believe that I know several people who, until I mentioned it, had no inkling that *The Lion, the Witch and the Wardrobe* had any bearing on Christian belief. The imagination transcends the doctrine. We relate and assent to the experiences and may afterwards find it at least interesting that they are based on a world-view that we would not accept if it were offered to us as non-fiction.

The imagination has become the authenticating element in the work, even if it was not originally so for the author. We are let into an experience via overtones, atmospheres and reverberations, via descants and delights, to the truth of which we submit simply as humans; we empathize with the writer's characters and the way they respond to what befalls them. We are, in some ways, beyond belief; in other ways, right in the thick of it.

If this were not so, I should, as a Christian, enjoy all

poetry written by other Christians – especially my contemporaries, for they live in the same world with the same
pressure, problems and difficulties. Actually the opposite
is the case, and the prospect of reading a book of modern
Christian poetry fills me with a kind of dread. Not because
I cannot assent to the doctrines that underpin the poems,
but because often there is little else but doctrine, unless it
be a kind of generalized (and therefore uninteresting) wash
of emotion or a tangle of jargon and cliché. Most people
would agree that the rules of Rugby School or of rugby
football do not become poetry simply because they are
written out in iambic pentameter, but they have not realized that the same is true of the gospels or the epistles of St
Paul.

Sincerity is not art; and art is not truth in the logical
scientific sense of the word.

So the artist, even when exploring his beliefs in *Animal
Farm* or *Four Quartets*, writes more engagingly and more
accessibly than he knows; the true reader, suspending his
disbelief, playing 'Let's Pretend' in this imaginary world,
gives more credit to unpalatable views than he might have
expected.

All writing is concerned with the nature of experience.
That is as true of a description of a moonlit garden as it
is of the book of Job, as it is of *Death of a Salesman*, 'I
wandered lonely as a cloud' or *The Mill on the Floss*. But
experience, it could be said, is neither here nor there
without some sort of exploration into the value of the
experience. And value in its turn depends on an implicit, if
not explicit, comparison with an accepted, understandable
ethos.

If, for instance, murder and betrayal were not the
heinous crimes they are, then the thriller would not grip us
as it does: we need an adequate spur to make our minds
and our consciences take notice. So, a piece of writing attains
its particular flavour, importance and significance – even its
shock-value – when set against the mind-set of the age

when it was written. To understand fully any work of literature, therefore, we must understand as much as we possibly can of the experience, the beliefs, the mind-set of those who were its first readers. If we do not do this, then we run the risk of misjudging what the writer was doing. If we compare him not with his own age but with our own experience and knowledge, we shall possibly find him quaint when he was being most serious and straightforward, naive when he was being ironic, and perceptive when he was merely repeating old and accepted formulas which we do not recognize.

But knowledge is always limited, ignorance is boundless. I have heard Alexander Pope dismissed for using *tired clichés* such as:

> Fools rush in where angels fear to tread

and

> A little learning is a dangerous thing

when, of course, it was Pope who coined these phrases and we who have dulled them with repetition and overuse and (worse) misquotation.

We may stop to wonder why Shakespeare begins Sonnet 130 with:

> My mistress' eyes are nothing like the sun

which is a kind of anti-metaphor. But if we take the trouble to read a few more poets of the sixteenth century we shall soon discover that it was a poetic commonplace to compare a woman's eyes with the sun. Shakespeare is being gently satirical at the expense of lesser poets as well as implying that his mistress is unique: literally and metaphorically incomparable.

To take another simple example, we shall miss some of the power of John Donne's:

> O my America! my new-found-land

(words with which he addresses his lover as she prepares

for bed) unless we remember that America had indeed been newly discovered and found to be a place of exotic beauty and apparently boundless treasure. Now, most of us will not have needed that history lesson, but how would we have fared when brought up against the Seven Sleepers, the mandrake and its supposed properties, words such as 'hydroptique', 'limbeck' and 'quintessence', all derived from the science of alchemy? And if we go back further in time we shall find much mediaeval poetry somewhat baffling if we do not understand the concept of courtly love.

The problem of fully understanding earlier texts is more often linguistic than conceptual. Words are continually changing their meanings, and this can create all sorts of pitfalls for the unwary or the unprepared reader.

If you don't know what the word 'atavistic' means, at least you know that you do not know and you can go and look it up in the dictionary. You can do the same with 'rhodomontade', 'serendipity' and 'teleological'. But what do you do when you meet the word 'sad' in this line from John Lydgate?

In youth be lusty, sad when thou art olde.

Most modern readers will not think twice, but be content to believe that Lydgate was advocating that the old should be unhappy, and on that basis may presume to judge Lydgate's opinions – even morality.

But the truth is that, at the time when the poem was written, the word 'sad' had not yet come to have the connotations it has for us today: it meant 'stable', 'firm', 'sound'. What today we might call 'balanced'. So in fact, Lydgate was contrasting the recklessness of youth with the settled maturity of age; a very different thing from what our reader would have concluded. Those who believe that age is sad (in our modern sense of the word) may still prefer that reading, and nobody can prevent them; but they must not confuse their whimsical invention with Lydgate's meaning.

Traps of this sort abound in English literature, certainly up to about a hundred years ago, and it is always the unsuspected word rather than the unknown word that is liable to mislead us. We are never quite safe. Roger McGough told me of an experience he had with the design of one of his book-jackets. Musicians, comedians and performance poets talk of 'gigs' rather than of 'shows' or 'performances' and, in a reference to this, he called one of his books *The Gig*. When the proofs arrived from the printer the illustration on the jacket showed a small two-wheeled carriage drawn by a horse. Very nice, but not what the man meant, and probably baffling to the reader.

All texts, and particularly old texts, need to be read very carefully, otherwise our understanding of them is liable to be partial, to say the least; based on a few points of emotional contact, some coincidence of autobiography or perception. A text becomes sentimentalized if we respond only to the bits that appeal to us rather than to the full picture that the writer has constructed.

The Bible offers us plenty of examples of this. Do we not prettify the narratives of the nativity? Have they not become, in the worst sense of the phrase, 'hallowed by time'? When we picture the stable, do we really smell the ammonia reek of the soaking straw underfoot, the piles of dung? Do we conveniently forget the rats and the spiders and the lice? Do we really take any account of the terror and pain of a young, inexperienced mother giving birth in the dark amid such squalor? Do we not see a barn rather than a stable – full of sweet-smelling hay and the gentle light of a lantern?

If that is so, then the meaning, indeed the glorious meaning, of the nativity has been allowed to swamp the truth of the event; and when that happens then even that meaning is no longer entirely true, it has been diminished.

When Jesus heals the man at the Pool of Bethesda in St John's Gospel, do we take away the comfortable sense of a nice man made whole and the picture – perhaps confirmed for us by the church drama group – of some altruistic middle-class people crying out in wonder and joy? Or do we really see decades of suffering and debility that cannot be assuaged by one miracle, even if a flash of hope may dazzle for a second; envy and an almost feral selfishness which has been engendered by a lifetime of anger, pain and despair? And all this topped off by the instant and ungrateful betrayal of Jesus to the authorities.

If we refuse to let our imagination work, then we are refusing the whole truth. We have been persuaded by the spirit of the age, by economists and scientists and experts of all kinds that the important thing about life is facts. Now, I like a good fact as well as anybody else, but I am not sure that there are as many around as people like to think. When we are dealing with life – as both religion and literature must do – facts are inextricable from the mind that perceives them, and that mind will be full of memories, associations, beliefs, ideas and experiences that we are essentially unable to share.

I went to Bridlington last week. That sounds pretty much like a fact, doesn't it? But it's not much of one. You will have to take my word for it. The chances are that nobody there will remember me, for they had no reason to. The tripmeter on my car will show that I travelled the requisite number of miles, but it won't prove my destination, and it may have been tampered with. Even for me the trip has changed from being a fact into being a memory, an experience. We can extend this further and point out that everything that has ever happened to us in our entire lives is now a memory, an experience that can only be recalled by means of the imagination. And this is as true of something that happened five minutes ago as of something that happened five years ago – or twenty-five.

The past is accessible only to our imagination.

As Christians we share a body of beliefs which we would not call vague or uncertain: they underpin everything we do, everything we are. And they can be tabulated, as they have been in the various creeds which we repeat in our different services. But we have come by our possession of those beliefs by very different ways and our understanding of them is more a product of our individuality than it is of our common ground. Even the creeds, those massive expressions of firm belief, are couched in metaphor. Try to unravel them into what is unambiguously factual and it will be found that even those truths which we hold to be primary and unshakeable can still be argued about.

By 'ascended into heaven' do you mean what I mean? How do you visualize 'ascended'? How do you see 'heaven'? What about 'descended into hell'? There are two big concepts for us to argue about. 'Sitteth at the right hand of the Father'. The problems pile up. The possible interpretations are multiplied.

It does not worry us. Or if it does it shouldn't. Life is not, as we have seen, nearly so much a matter of fact as of faith, experience, memory and imagination. Matters of true importance are inexpressible and unprovable except through the imagination working on language and language somehow chiming with experience.

It is the writer's job to make sense of and to find pattern in a seemingly random world. Part of that pattern will involve beliefs about why and how, which is the realm of religious exploration. If the pattern of words and symbols and images is truthful enough for us to give imaginative assent to the world that the writer has created, we are able to meet and understand (even if, in the end, we reject) beliefs which are strange, unexamined or even uncongenial.

When we look back at the whole of English literature we shall find that, in the matter of understanding the spiritual standpoint from which it was written, the Christian has a distinct and indeed enviable advantage over all other readers, however scholarly. The beliefs which formed such a substantial part of the world-view of the majority of writers up to the present day are his beliefs too. To have a belief, to have had something proved upon your pulse, is without doubt the best and deepest way to understand the writings of those who have committed themselves to the same ideals, the same concept of the universe and its governance; not the only way, but the safest way.

The historian Barbara W. Tuchman points out:

> Difficulty of empathy, of genuinely entering into the mental and emotional values of the Middle Ages, is the final obstacle. The main barrier is, I believe, the Christian religion as it then was: the matrix and law of medieval life, omnipresent, indeed, compulsory. Its insistent principle that the life of the spirit and of the afterworld was superior to the here and now, to material life on earth, is one that the modern world does not share.
>
> (Tuchman, *A Distant Mirror*, Foreword, p. xix)

For her, the gap between the ideal and the actual does not demonstrate a kind of Christian hypocrisy, and she criticizes Gibbon for implying that it does. The Christian ideal, she says,

> must represent a need, something more fundamental than Gibbon's 18th century enlightenment allowed for, or his elegant ironies could dispose of. While I recognize its presence, it requires a more religious bent than mine to identify with it.
>
> (Tuchman, op. cit.)

She is talking specifically about the fourteenth century. We may go back further and say that from *Beowulf*, in the form in which we have it, right up to the present day, the world-view of by far the greater part of those who gave us our literature has been a Christian one. As we briefly discussed in chapter 6, even those who consciously rejected a Christian world-view knew clearly what they were arguing with and what they were rejecting; they were still writing against a sharply definable background of opinion and belief. They knew the Bible; their minds were steeped in its imagery, its rhythms, its incidents, its characters. Moreover, and this is important, especially when considering the influence of the Bible on their writing, they all knew the *same* Bible – the Authorized Version after its publication in 1611. Before that there was a choice of versions including those of Wyclif, Tyndale and Coverdale as well, of course, as the Vulgate. The AV was a consciously traditional translation – deliberately not a new version – which means that it is very close to the Bible that all European writers had been familiar with for centuries.

I shall almost certainly upset true biblical scholars if I suggest that there was little difference between these various versions, but it is demonstrable that 90 per cent of Tyndale's work was taken over into the AV, and the point I wish to make is that they are much more stylistically and rhythmically in agreement than any of them is with a modern translation. If we wish to make a true comparison between the Bible and the use made of it by an author of the past, we should be foolish to use the Good News Bible or the NIV.

If we read and know the Bible, then, the poetry of the past will be accessible to us in a way that it can never be to the person who is ignorant of scripture. Northrop Frye, in *The Great Code*, talks of when he began to teach literature in universities:

> I soon realized that a student of English literature who does not know the Bible does not understand a good deal of what is going on in what he reads; the most conscientious student will be continually misconstruing the implications, even the meaning.
>
> (Frye, *The Great Code*, Introduction, p. xii)

But if, in addition to reading and knowing, we can believe and give personal assent, not only will the literature become accessible but so will a great deal of the mind and the character of the author. Sympathy and empathy spring across the centuries, and we can become a true audience for the work, not just a classifier of its genre or of its linguistic sophistication.

The loss of a common background of accepted belief has been lamented by T. S. Eliot and others, and it has made a great difference to the way literature is written as well as the way in which it is read. But for the Christian community that ethos is still there; the thread remains unbroken. A text may still have value as well as interest, may convey wisdom as well as delight. That is literature performing its proper function.

10

*Go search this thing**

———⊸⊸———

If one reads what writers say about critics, or even what critics say about other critics, it soon becomes clear that the business of criticism, of judging and assessing a literary text, is a difficult one which has not yet been fully fathomed. General theories fail because they are general theories and not stringent enough to say anything really useful. Watertight theories fail because they refuse to let in lifegiving water – they grow quickly, even spectacularly, but then they wither at the roots. Criticism made solely on the basis of some political (with a large or a small 'p') or religious belief finds itself necessarily speechless or irrelevant when it comes to dealing with the huge mass of literature that happens not to be addressing such issues.

The basis of literature, as this book has tried to demonstrate, is life; it rests on an individual response to experience filtered through the imagination. For a poet, as Eliot famously pointed out in 'East Coker', each new poem is a new beginning, a completely fresh leap in the dark, an attempt to bring meaningful sound out of a vast silence. Any critical theory must take this into consideration.

And yet a writer writes within a tradition whether he likes it or not. I cannot write a poem as if Shakespeare, Yeats, Ted Hughes or Robert Frost had never put pen to paper. Every new poem, every new novel, may be a leap in

---

* Herbert: 'The Method'

the dark, but it has to shoulder its way into the multitude of existing works and find its own place. It may match what surrounds it or it may be in stark contrast, but it cannot be seen in isolation.

There seems to be a problem here to start with, or at least a tension: how do we reconcile the utter newness of a new poem with the fact that it is still just another poem?

Perhaps our image of a leap into the dark needs to be refined, for the darkness is not entirely dark; it is full of dancing lights which have been lit by other writers. Some are exquisite little candles, some are vast arc lights; some illuminate huge areas rather dimly, some cast a clear, pure light on one tiny detail. The challenge for the writer is to add to all this illumination; to choose a dark spot for his particular lantern or to set up his looking-glass so that it may reflect existing light into new areas; it may even be to blow out candles that are guttering or casting grotesque and misleading shadows and to replace them with something that gleams more warmly, more steadily.

What the critic has to do (apart from writing 'see me' against this interminable metaphor) is twofold. He must judge whether the lantern is an adequate lantern with a well-trimmed wick, clean glass and pure oil; and he must also consider whether its light is performing any useful function. These are distinct and discrete processes.

Let us – to everyone's relief – abandon the metaphor and come back to discussing works of literature. When faced with a novel or a poem, the critic's first job is to assess it purely as a novel or a poem. That is – to pick out a few simple examples – to determine whether it has an internal integrity or whether it is working against itself in some way, whether the imagery works or appears false, trite or too esoteric; whether the parts work in relation to the whole; whether it is too allusive, not allusive enough, too repetitive or not repetitive enough; whether its obscurity is necessary or the result of chaotic thought or garbled syntax; whether its simplicity is effective or banal. And all these judgements will be made, not according to some non-existent perfection that the critic has dreamed up and against which ideal every work has to be measured on a sliding scale, but according to the rules and expectations that the poem or novel has laid down for itself.

This is where the critic has to treat the poem or the novel as a unique, new creation with its own pattern and logic; a work to be taken on its own terms. This is the sort of process that I was going through with Larkin's 'Absences' in chapter 7, albeit in a very hasty and superficial way. Everything that was said about the poem was from internal evidence, not from some archetypal idea of what a poem *ought* to be.

It is necessary to stress this because it is very easy to blame a poet for not writing the poem you expected or would really have preferred. Unless you understand what the poem is trying to be and what the author was up to, you can even end up by criticizing as faults the very effects that the author was at great pains to achieve. We should be rightly disappointed in Hardy's artistic integrity if in *Far from the Madding Crowd* a cow were to lean over the hedge and offer even an extremely perceptive comment about farmer Boldwood or Sergeant Troy. Animals, we tell ourselves with an assurance born of long experience, do not talk. How right we are; but how foolish we should look if we were to bring the same criterion to bear on Beatrix Potter or *The Wind in the Willows*. As human beings, we may be entitled to say 'This doesn't happen.' As critics, the most we can say is, 'This doesn't happen in *this* kind of book.'

It may seem extreme to suggest that a critic would be so foolish as to expect from Beatrix Potter what he would expect from Hardy, but the history of criticism is full of bad judgements on a similar pattern. Milton is blamed for not being Herbert, Pope is blamed for not being Shelley, de la Mare is blamed for not being Ezra Pound. The antidote to such a critical disease is to rejoice in the prodigious variety of English literature and to try and discover the individuality, the uniqueness of each writer. But both of these qualities can only truly be known by comparison. We do not need anything other than the poem alone to tell whether or not it *works*; but if we are to decide whether it is good or not, whether it is distinctive or not, we need more information.

Even though it may have its own internal integrity, it might be unremarkable in terms of what other writers have attempted, or even in terms of what this particular writer has done before. Is it merely a repetition of his own or some other writer's formula? And, if it is, has it brought improvement? Every piece of work has a pedigree. Let us take the narrative poem as an example. Even if we omit the first two most famous examples, *Beowulf* and *Sir Gawain and the Green Knight*, on the grounds that they are written in what amounts to a different language, we still have examples from writers as diverse as Chaucer, Marlowe, Milton, Keats, Coleridge, Wordsworth, Scott, Byron, Morris, Longfellow, Hardy, Browning, Masefield, Elizabeth Bishop, Watkins, MacDiarmid, Levi, W. S. Graham and dozens of others. They will have solved problems, invented techniques, failed in some experiments and succeeded in others. It would be as silly not to take their achievements into consideration when dealing with a new poem as it would for an aircraft designer still to be running off clifftops flapping his arms.

'This is good' and 'I like this' are different sorts of judgement; not, of course, incompatible, any more than 'This is good but I do not like it,' but different. We shall come on to the question of liking in a moment. The first thing, however, that a critic needs if he is to offer sound and valuable judgements about any piece of writing, is to be acquainted with as much literature as possible, in as many different genres and from as many different ages as possible. Otherwise what is he to say that is genuinely helpful, when Mr X offers him this – the first line of his latest poem?

How like a winter has this summer been.

Technical knowledge alone will allow him to say that this is a line of iambic pentameter – five *feet* or units, each consisting of one unstressed (∪) and one stressed (–) sylla-ble – with the first foot reversed (– ∪ instead of ∪ –) and, depending on where the reader thinks the emphasis ought to be laid, with the third foot perhaps reversed as well. That is, either:

$$\overline{\text{How}} \ \underset{\smile}{\text{like}} \ \Big| \ \underset{\smile}{a} \ \underset{\smile}{\text{win}} \ \Big| \ \underset{\smile}{\text{ter}} \ \overline{\text{has}} \ \Big| \ \underset{\smile}{\text{this}} \ \overline{\text{sum}} \ \Big| \ \underset{\smile}{\text{mer}} \ \overline{\text{been}}$$

or

$$\overline{\text{How}} \ \underset{\smile}{\text{like}} \ \Big| \ \underset{\smile}{a} \ \overline{\text{win}} \ \Big| \ \underset{\smile}{\text{ter}} \ \underset{\smile}{\text{has}} \ \Big| \ \underset{\smile}{\text{this}} \ \overline{\text{sum}} \ \Big| \ \underset{\smile}{\text{mer}} \ \overline{\text{been}}.$$

He might also say that the sense of melancholy implicit in the words finds an appropriate echo in the long vowel sounds which are slow and dark, and yet which are varied enough not to draw the attention to the technique. The art that conceals art. The line, he might add, has to be read fairly slowly, it does not trip along, and thus signals quite clearly that this is to be a considered and meditative poem: not a silly squib, probably not a satire.

If the critic is a bit more perceptive, he will wonder about the collision of the 's' sounds in the phrase 'this summer'. How should this be read? Do you join up the s of 'this' with the s of 'summer' as you would in ordinary everyday speech so that what comes out is 'thissummer'? There is then a risk that it might be heard as 'the summer'. Or do you make a break between the two words and articulate each s separately, which is not only difficult but sounds artificial and over-precise?

And then, just as he is feeling pleased with all these perceptive comments, a better-read critic comes along and points out that perhaps we should refrain from too much praise until we have also noted that the line is a direct pinch from Sonnet 97 by Shakespeare:

How like a winter hath my absence been . . .

And that puts an entirely new complexion on the whole

matter. We then have to decide whether this is sheer dis-honesty at work, or literary allusion, and we need to see the rest of that poem before we can decide.

Because the techniques of pure literary criticism would take hundreds of pages to explain and discuss, and because hundreds – indeed thousands – of pages have been written on the subject by other writers, but mainly because any reader who has picked up this book is probably more interested in a rather different kind of discussion, I shall content myself with saying just a couple more things about this first function of the critic before I turn to the more difficult and more contentious area of his second function: the discussion of a work's value.

One thing in particular I do not want to do, or even appear to do, and that is to elevate the process of criticism above the process of reading and enjoying. Literature is a living creature, and the only way it can truly stay alive is in the heart and soul of a delighted reader. I do not happen to think that dissecting it and studying its elements and its workings will do it any harm. The real harm comes when people think or act as if that were all it were fit for: a corpse to be kept in a morgue called 'Culture' and brought out and defrosted from time to time for the purposes of inspection and instruction.

The true virtue of literature is to be discovered in the small space that includes the book and the reader's brain; and the highest praise that any author can hear is the simple statement: 'I love this book.' But anyone who makes that statement will not want to stop there, and others who also love books will always greet it with the question, 'Why?' Even the smallest critical vocabulary helps us to say more than the rather unsatisfactory, 'Well, I just do.' Books that are anything more than mental chewing gum or blatant fantasy-fulfilment will always provoke discussion and comparison, will lead to reading more books, better books, deeper books, making new discoveries, finding more and more nourishment and challenge for both the mind and the spirit.

It is unfortunate that a great deal of academic discourse today – and, therefore, I'm afraid, pseudo-academic discourse too – has become an end in itself, arid and solipsistic. Somewhere along the line it has been forgotten that writers write in order to be understood and enjoyed. Occasionally even this has been denied: some of the more extreme forms of deconstruction deny the writer any conscious control, meaning or possibility of reference to anything beyond the text itself. Now, as far as meaning and reference are concerned there is no essential difference between an utterance in literature and an utterance in ordinary social and intellectual speech, which makes one wonder what kind of moral universe such critics inhabit. It is true that critics and writers have always argued about some things and no doubt they always will, but surely a critical stance that would have been unacceptable and indeed intolerable to every writer must need a little bit of revision.

Once it would have been true to say that the critic served the text; nowadays it is the text that serves the critic.

Because any critic's main tool in elucidating the meaning and the distinctive flavour of a text is comparison, there is always going to be a temptation to carry comparison to extremes and build up a kind of league table of writers or, even worse, of individual works. It is a fruitless enterprise: one that will appeal rather to a merely tidy mind than to an intelligent one. Human nature will ensure that such a list will reveal very few objective standards and very many personal blind spots. Taste and value are not absolutes. Nor is technique; what works in an epic by Milton will not work in a lyric by Graves. Some works, such as Tennyson's *In Memoriam*, spoke deeply and powerfully to a certain age and have less power to the general mass of readers today. There are still, though, individuals – and I am one of them – who find it a superb and fascinating poem.

Hierarchies are unnecessary and misleading. I do not enjoy *In Memoriam* any less because *King Lear* is, in most people's opinion, better; Seamus Heaney's carrying off the Nobel Prize for Literature isn't going to stop me reading

John Burnside; and I refuse to stop enjoying the particular felicities of Edna St Vincent Millay just because critical opinion would have me admit that Wallace Stevens is greater. The construction of league tables implies a kind of touchstone of excellence against which all poems of all ages and of all styles may be measured, whereas actually the opposite is true: it is only by looking at the poems that have been written and passed down to us that we have any idea of what a poem is.

If we are to be critics ourselves, the other thing we should think about is the language that it is appropriate for a critic to use. While there are honourable exceptions to this generalization, we have become used to the sort of criticism that tells us a great deal about the critic and a rather meagre amount about the work that is under scrutiny. Words are used not for their preciseness but for their quality as invective or, less frequently, compliment.

What is needed is an adequate summary of how a writer has tackled the job he has set himself; where and why he succeeds, where and why he fails. Such a summary needs to be focused and specific, but all too often we get vague words and vogue words, waffle and self-display which, it is tempting to conclude, are there to cloak the ignorance of the critic or his lack of homework.

What, for instance, do we learn when we are told that a book is 'rather provincial' in its outlook? The word 'provincial' is used, almost without exception, as a vaguely deprecatory term. Yet the true strength of Hardy's novels resides in their specifically provincial quality. The whole point about Jude, abut Giles Winterbourne, about Diggory Venn and Gabriel Oak is that they were not members of the metropolitan chattering classes, they were uneducated and – in Hardy's terms – undefiled by the values of the world beyond their province. A moment's thought will be enough to remind us that the provincial is one of the great informing elements in English literature as a whole; our most valued authors are the most provincial. Philip Larkin built his whole reputation on his distance from the centre of things, on the massive significance of the unremarkable. A long list is not necessary to make the point; suffice it to say that Vaughan, Herbert, Swift, Trollope, Bennett, Austen, Wordsworth, R. S. Thomas, Ted Hughes, John Clare, Charles Causley, Laurie Lee and Lawrence Sterne, as well as the dozens of names you have come up with yourself, find their defining strength and individuality in the very quality which is condemned by the world 'provincial'.

There are other words which fall into the same category: 'adolescent', for instance, 'vulgar' and 'bourgeois'. They do not define, they do not explain; in fact, the only thing they communicate at all is the message 'I am angry' or, even worse, 'I feel myself to be superior.' It is worth remembering that J. D. Salinger's *The Catcher in the Rye* was received with great acclaim and has become a modern classic. It could, without a word of a lie, be described as adolescent, provincial and bourgeois.

You will seldom, if ever, find such loose and unhelpful terminology in the writing of true critics, but the non-specialist seldom reads the true critics. The weekly or even daily newspaper review has become the source of our information about new books, and these reviews, though they are sometimes written by genuine critics with a wide knowledge and a genuine love of literature, tend to be the work of journalists who very often see it as their function to write not a balanced and thoughtful piece but an entertaining and provocative piece where all the wit and energy is for the sake of clever writing or self-display rather than being channelled into finding truthful insights.

We should be careful, then, when choosing our words. 'Bad', 'dull', 'inept', 'trite', 'amorphous'; these are all words that can be used because they convey something a little more specific. They all need further explanation, of course. What is trite about the book? The ideas? The phraseology? The dialogue? In what way is it dull? Is it repetitive? Have we heard it all before? Are the characters unsympathetic? Are the sentences too short, too long, or all constructed in the same way? If you are honest about what you believe to be the true quality of the book, then further questions of this sort will clarify and focus the criticism, make it less like a growl and more like an argument. After all, one cannot argue with feelings, only with findings. Feelings are unprovable, but what the text says and how it says it are verifiable facts. We must always start there.

Now, I think, we are able to go a step further and discuss the second function of the critic – beyond description, beyond analysis and into the realm of value. Given that the text does this, this and this, and does it in this particular way, was it worth it? Is it communicating anything of value? It is here that the most interesting and the most difficult discussions begin. The values that we, as men and women, hold will determine the amount of value we can ascribe to various works of literature. But let us always remember that this is a different operation from judging the work as literature. A novel may be most wonderfully constructed, full of brilliantly drawn characters speaking rich dialogue in a beautifully paced narrative, full of intrigue, humour, excitement and insight; and yet we may find it morally repugnant. This good book is a bad book.

That sounds like a paradox, but it is not; I have merely juxtaposed two completely different types of judgement. As critics we must keep them separate. We must praise the artist for his consummate skill as an artist, for that is only fair; it is honest *literary* criticism. We may then go on to censure him as a man and as a moralist, but that is a separate judgement from the literary one. The literary judgement may lay bare the values that D. H. Lawrence or Kipling or Pope upheld; but it is a different kind of judgement that goes on to say whether they were admirable values or true values and whether we too should uphold them.

The Christian has to be very careful here. He may be tempted to dismiss a book that does not discuss the relationship between man and his God as valueless; thus missing, perhaps, the important issues and truths that are explored: human love, coming to terms with grief, our responsibility to the rest of creation, personal integrity and political pressure, and so forth. He may, on the other hand, be inveigled into praising a book unduly because it is written by a Christian writer and fail to notice that it is manipulative, untrue to life and so vaguely spiritual that it offers merely a New Age wishy-washy hopefulness rather than a discerning analysis of the problem. Such an error can usually be avoided if a stringent literary judgement is made first and is kept distinct from any mitigation we may be inclined to allow on the grounds that the writer 'has his heart in the right place'. It is a writer's job to put his pen in the right places. If he does not do that, we shall hardly be able to discover where his heart is.

So let us dismiss the mistaken hypothesis that Christian = Good, Secular = Bad. It is this sort of thinking that leads all too easily to cruel and impertinent criticism. The Christian imagines that he has felt the burning coal on his lips; he is the agent and spokesman of God; with the approval of his own pure conscience and a couple of thousand years of history, he spits and fulminates, and even the grain of truth that may have been there to start with is blown away by the force of his own wind. We do well to remember the words of the man whose lips *were* touched by the burning coal:

> For my thoughts are not your thoughts, neither are your ways my ways, saith the Lord. For as the heavens are higher than the earth, so are my ways higher than your ways, and my thoughts than your thoughts.
>
> (Isaiah 55. 8–9)

The writer can never work as Jesus Christ, and we should not expect him to. A literary text is not a sermon, nor is it a piece of evangelism. Its value lies not in the answers it gives, for it will probably not give answers; its value is in the questions it asks, the trains of thought it leads us into, the possibilities it envisages. It is doubtful whether the writer will even work as St John the Baptist, for, though he may be a voice crying in the wilderness, he will more often make us see just how crooked the path is than make it straight. The most a Christian writer can do, perhaps, is, by being honest to his personal experience – perhaps even his experience of doubt rather than of faith – effect the spread of an imaginative and intellectual climate favourable to the entertaining of Christian ideas. The history of English literature alone is enough to demonstrate that there are people of not negligible moral and intellectual calibre who can take such ideas seriously enough to live by them.

Centuries ago St Augustine reminded us that the truth is the truth and it belongs to God and needs to be recognized as the truth wherever it may be found. Centuries before that, Jesus had remarked that the faith of a Roman soldier was greater than he had found among the Jews. We should not need any greater authority for the possibility that we too may find God's truth, God's prompting and even God's teaching among the works of unbelievers.

But at the same time, we must not sell our souls to the unbelievers; we must not, unthinkingly, accept secular standards and secular opinions. A technique is a technique and a skill is a skill, whether it be displayed by a heathen or by a Christian, but our values are not so transferable. In the end, all our judgements, all our criticisms and appreciations must be based on what God has taught us about our relationship to him, to one another and to the whole of creation. He has taught us these things not only through the example of Christ but through everything he has put in our way: friends and families, enemies and strangers, hopes and disappointments, delights and fears, sheer, unadulterated happiness and sheer, unadulterated anguish, our certainties and our doubts.

Just as these things will have informed the writings of our poets and novelists, whether they acknowledge it as such or whether they see it as mere circumstance, so the critic is entitled to bring his beliefs and his view of the universe to bear on the value and significance of a text. A book is something created by a human being to give delight and enlightenment to another human being. If it does neither, or does one at the expense of the other, the reader, in his capacity as critic, is entitled to say so.

One of the things that might prevent him from doing so is a fear of appearing ignorant or unfashionable. Now it is not helpful for a critic to be ignorant, that's true; but it is not such a terrible disability as one might think. Yes, the person who has read a hundred novels will have more to work with than the person who has read three, but intelligence is not entirely dependent on knowledge.

Earlier in this chapter we discussed how a poem (you may substitute book if you wish) has to be seen in two ways which are in some respects opposites: it is a new, individual, independent creation and, at the same time, it is part of a long tradition which started over a thousand years ago. To see it as a part of the whole picture you need a certain amount of knowledge, but intelligence is all you need in order to explain why a book works, why it is humane and valuable, or indeed why it is shallow and dangerous.

When we come to the fear of being unfashionable we are on even safer ground. Fashion is the scourge of literary criticism; it is the scourge of all criticism of all the arts. At the same time it is the most insidious of all influences, and perhaps we can never be entirely free of it, but whatever else fashion is, it is always, to a certain extent, accidental and it is always ephemeral. It can, therefore, be nothing to do with the intrinsic value of the work in question. That has remained constant, it is our view of it that has changed.

Tastes alter, new techniques and forms are invented, fresh ideas come to our attention, and this is all to the good, for otherwise we should be stuck in a rut and our art would be condemned to repeat stale old formulae harping on a few ideas in a few fairly predictable ways.

But if tastes change they may sometimes change from the deep to the shallow, from the complex to the simple, from the significant to the trite. In a nutshell, they may change for the worse. It would be a very optimistic person who could look back over the whole history of the world and declare that every change had been a change for the better; and the same is true of literature.

Whatever we think of Wordsworth's poetry, we must admit, with the benefit of hindsight, that his deliberate and reasoned departure from the diction of his predecessors and his use of 'the very language of men' rather than an artificial – or what he saw as an artificial – and elevated vocabulary, changed the nature and the scope of English poetry in a dramatic and lasting way. That much is certain. But the important point is that, even if we approve, we must not be tempted to dismiss or ignore the sort of poetry that he thought was in need of refreshment. There is still plenty to admire in the poetry of the eighteenth century, and plenty for the twentieth-century writers to learn from, if only in the matter of sheer craft and discipline.

It is a great pity, but it seems to be a universal rule that the new must always supersede the old and render it obsolete and, to all intents and purposes, valueless. Why can it never take its place alongside? Be an addition to the old rather than an alternative? The answer is *fashion*. Fashion works like that, and the only consolation is that the whirligig of time will bring in his revenges; unfairness will tend to get straightened out, but not usually for a while.

One would think, for instance, that it was a fairly simple task for a musician to decide whether Arnold Bax was or was not a good symphonist. His problem, or one of his problems, was an almost exact contemporary called Arnold Schoenberg who halfway through Bax's career began writing music of a sort that had never been heard before. First of all it was atonal – dispensing with a key or a harmonic centre – and then, later, it was written according to a system Schoenberg invented himself, whereby every note in the chromatic scale was given equal importance. Since there are twelve notes in the chromatic scale it was called twelve-note music. For some people this music was extraordinarily exciting, iconoclastic, revolutionary, forward-looking. Even those who hated it wouldn't disagree, though they might agree regretfully. This was the new music. Bax's luscious harmonies, massive canvases and sometimes painterly impressionism were suddenly old hat. He had been overtaken; he was *passé*; he was outmoded. And because enthusiasm will brook no reservations, and because keeping up with the Joneses has always been attractive to the less contemplative mind, and because there is as much partisanship in the arts as there is in football, you couldn't like Bax any more without being disparaged.

The twelve-note revolution has died down, of course. Now the thought police are out to make sure we prize the minimalists: Glass, Tavener, Gorecki, and so on. Meanwhile, for those who love music rather than jumping on band-wagons, Bax and others of his cast of mind, Holst, Moeran, Warlock and Finzi, are beginning to be rediscovered and played again.

The pre-Raphaelite painters were, no so long ago, fit only for biscuit tins and chocolate boxes; now they are allowed their place in the history of English painting, and it is not an unimportant one.

What seems to have happened in all these cases is a confusion between the two functions of the critic. Value and integrity or value and skill have been mixed up. Because we no longer were interested in listening to Bax, he was no longer a 'good' composer. Because we were rather keen on being unemotional, the rather strong emotions aroused by the pre-Raphaelites meant they were not 'good' painters. It could, of course, be argued that the disregard of Bax came because we had consciously rejected the values that his music seemed to be communicating and the natural world that was its main inspiration. Alternatively, it could have been that we had so fully taken on these values and assented to them that he no longer had anything to say to us. It would be an interesting argument but a hard one to uphold. No society has truly rejected nature or been uninterested in the realm of myth and legend that so attracted Bax; and the delight of hearing someone formulate beautifully and memorably values that we hold ourselves is one of the prime attractions of art – it is hardly likely to be the reason for his neglect.

The great thing about all the arts is that you don't have to renounce one thing in order to enjoy another. You can enjoy Pope *and* Wordsworth, Bax *and* Schoenberg. To enjoy the summer pudding you don't have to vilify the casserole or refuse the cheese.

Let us, as honest critics, refuse to be led by the nose by the latest fad; let us base our judgements on something more reliable than the clock or the perhaps ill-informed opinions of others who may have an image to preserve, an ignorance to cloak or even a powerful employer to keep sweet. Let us dare to see novelty for what it is and authenticity for what it is, and not be afraid to lament the first when it does not serve the second. While we must beware that our unfashionable stance does not itself turn into a fashion or a pose, we should dare to be as honest and vulnerable as the small boy in the Hans Christian Andersen story who stood up in public and against the world and shouted the simple truth: 'But the Emperor is not wearing any clothes!'

The Zeitgeist, the spirit of the age, is a strong force, but one which is very difficult to pin down. It is a kind of way of thinking, and, as such, lies one degree behind fashion and dictates the sort of fashions that will find favour. In the 1930s the Zeitgeist was a sense of disillusioned cynicism of the sort that informed the poetry of Auden, MacNeice, Spender and Empson, among others. In the 1960s it was a sort of gentle lawlessness which we now call permissiveness; individual desires were seen as more important than conformity to rules, written or unwritten; authority was suspect. The literature of the period was experimental, iconoclastic and sometimes individual to the point of obscurity.

If we look at the history of the period, it is not difficult to see why such a feeling was abroad. In the 1930s Hitler was rising as the memories of the First World War were still vivid, and Spain was fighting a civil war in which many English writers involved themselves. Similarly, the permissiveness of the 1960s can be seen as a reaction to the austerities and duties imposed by the Second World War. The end of food rationing was followed by the end of freedom rationing. We can look back, too, to the seventeenth century and see the morbid, death-obsessed atmosphere generated by many of the Jacobean dramatists as the reaction to the expanding universe of the Elizabethans: powerful, vital and, apparently, invincible.

It is more difficult to recognize clearly the spirit of the age while you are still living through the age in question. But the attempt should be made, especially by Christians, for the temptation is to believe that, as a Christian, one is immune to such influences. That is not self-evident.

Certainly the spirit of the age tends always to work towards imbalance by preferring and emphasizing one thing (even one good thing) above all else, and the true Christian will be intent on redressing and restoring balance. But the spirit of the age is also at work in the churches. Where people are trailing from meeting to meeting, clamouring for 'power healing' to be manifest or for laughter to flatten them, they are clamouring less for justice and righteousness, they are not feeding the poor. Where Christians grind themselves into a shadow in their work with the homeless and the addicted, they may become grimly judgemental to the point of refusing God's refreshment and healing power. As we saw in chapter 8, Christ should be central, not one aspect of his work, or a kind of fanaticism is almost bound to follow – and the worst kind of sin: sincere sin. Mercy is sentimental without justice; justice is cruel without mercy. The balance always has to be kept.

We need to be on our guard against conformity to the spirit of the age, whether that conformity be blatant and deliberate or whether it be unwitting. In many books and films a pseudo-morality is quietly smuggled in. Right and wrong are no longer absolutes or even up for discussion; instead, what is right is determined by the desires of the hero or heroine, what is wrong is anything that counters those desires. The fact that there is a pseudo-morality rather than none at all helps to blind us to the fact that it is pseudo. Accept it, and all sorts of confusion follows. It is no longer good versus evil but self versus everything else; yet, owing to our sympathy for the protagonists, it feels like good versus evil.

The writer and director Murray Watts, as part of one of the many talks he gives about the relationship between Christianity and the arts, especially theatre, television and film, wrote a powerful piece entitled *Credo* which was delivered by three actors. The first of its three sections is spoken by an Angel of Light and it reveals the cynical forces at work in some aspects of the media. Talking of a hero and heroine, he tells us:

> I will enrich their characters at every turn at the expense of others.

> If they commit adultery I will not allow you to enter deeply into the lives of their victims, I will drain these other characters of life, of humour, I will make them ciphers, ridiculous stereotypes; I will show you how such shallow fools clearly deserve to be cheated and deceived . . .

> I will offer you edited highlights of the spiritual world, God's world, speeches about justice, war, love, forgiveness, moments of moral insight, jewels of inspiration; in such a way that you will never notice how many people were killed in the name of justice, how many families were ruined in the name of love.

> You will laugh, perfectly on cue . . . when I cuckold yet another bald-headed old fool or uptight, uncaring wife. You will applaud when more faceless, character-less extras are amusingly blown to smithereens.

One does not have to pile up the evidence. It is interesting that even a film as gently humane and generally restrained in its treatment of violence as *The Shawshank Redemption* has to pile wrong upon wrong in order to come up with its right, has to avoid us asking certain questions in order to achieve our satisfaction at the ending. It would be churlish to carp unduly at a film which is head and shoulders above many others that could be mentioned, but the use of the word 'redemption' for what happens is, to say the least, interesting when compared with the ideas of redemption in, say, *The Winter's Tale*, *Paradise Regained* or C. S. Lewis' science-fiction trilogy; not to mention the novels of that marvellous and bafflingly underrrated author Charles Williams.

There are no certain methods to avoid the influence of the Zeitgeist or to recognize its distortions, and the Christian critic must avoid becoming just a differently motivated member of the thought police. A useful stratagem, however, is to resolve, as C. S. Lewis advocated, that for every contemporary novel you read you should read one old novel or one book of poetry written before you were born. What this will do, since the writers of these books will have started with a different set of presuppositions from our contemporaries (either subtly different or radically different, depending on how far back you choose to go), is help you to gain a perspective on style and content and hidden agendas; help you to differentiate more surely between what is of the age, what is of the author and what is of eternity. Authenticity will soon shine out from what is mere superficiality or self-display. There are no 'right' or 'wrong' opinions; only opinions that can be substantiated and opinions that cannot – that are mere personal whims. Like T. S. Eliot, though, I should be very suspicious of a reader whose opinions coincided precisely and at all points with the judgement of the ages and who only found satisfaction in the demonstrably first-rate; just as I should be suspicious of somebody who could find nothing of value or interest in what the world has, by general consent, thought to be our greatest geniuses. Both positions smack of a self-conscious pose. Man cannot live by caviare and smoked salmon alone; nor can he live healthily on scraps.

One of the things that such a method of reading will very soon make clear is the implications that follow from the decay of a shared ethos, a publicly stated system of belief. To put it another way, the world-view of the twentieth century is a dozen world-views, a score, a hundred. That there is no accepted authority for our thoughts or our behaviour, and that, therefore, morality is simply a matter of pragmatism, has thrown into confusion such matters as criminal justice, individual rights, welfare and the health services, particularly in relation to abortion and euthanasia. Some would say that this is an excellent thing and will lead to a reconsideration of first principles; but in a society where there is no agreed authority for our morals except that atrophied organ our individual conscience, where everything is relative, where do we go to find those first principles? To temper what is still, in essence, a Christian-inspired legal system with what we like to think of as rationality is never going to be satisfactory. Whose rationality? That of the reactionary conservative or of the wishy-washy liberal? Who decides? And on what first principles?

We may seem to have come a long way from novels, plays and poetry, but these problems have an influence on the Christian writer. How do you solve the problem of writing the book you want to write when you feel, at the same time, that there is no audience for it? When you know that half your readers will dismiss it if it smacks of the old Judeo-Christian philosophy that the present century has tried to shake off, and the other half will reject it if it is not reducible to a message, and preferably an evangelistic one? Does anybody, actually, share your world-view?

There are no easy answers, and certainly no foolproof ones. But part of the answer is that if you write well and, before trying to assert or explain any particular religious conviction, are faithful to the demands of the form you are dealing with, then you have a very good chance of success. As we saw in the previous chapter, the imaginative framework is the important thing; if you get that right and you remain true to your vision of the work rather than to some putative canon of 'soundness' or 'acceptability', you will have done all you can. To judge from the novels I have read or been sent, pandering to the Christian subculture and making the right noises in the acceptable jargon is the sure-fire road to failure.

There is a lot of truth in the old adage: 'Love God and do what you like.' There are times, and when you are writing is one of them, when you must trust to the Spirit within you and, in the best way possible, take God for granted. Dare to shrug off a feeling of responsibility; dare to believe that the future of Chistendom does not depend on your novel or your poem, but remember that your immortal soul may well be tied up with the honesty and truthfulness of your vision.

This has not been a book designed for those who want to be writers (though I hope it will not be without interest for such people), but a book to begin exploring how literature works and how it can illuminate our faith; how it can lead us gently into the safe darkness like a lantern, or show us, with perhaps a shock of clarity, as in a looking-glass, our own struggling selves.

But I should like to end with a word about the necessity of a Christian contribution to literature. We must continue to tell our stories, to explore our experience of those vast abstracts such as love and death and mercy and sacrifice and forgiveness and redemption in concrete fictions that can shake the mind and the heart. For, in the end, there is nothing else worth talking about. Man's relationship to the universe and to his God, the actual compared to the ideal, is the stuff of all comedy and all tragedy, and the Christian voice should echo through literature, through the nation's memory, as loudly as any other.

For most of the latter part of this century Christian involvement in literature, in film and in television has been of a fairly negative kind. Christians have not been at the forefront or anywhere near the forefront of artistic endeavour and development; they are the ones who stand sulkily in the background, muttering and complaining. Some men ask probing questions; Christians give pat answers. Some men make things; Christians try to ban things. Some men create; Christians censure. Some men stride out and colonize; Christians withdraw and sermonize.

There are honest enough heathens around writing extremely well, but who kept them honest? There are other heathens writing dangerous nonsense. And which is better: to mutter and shake our heads and complain, or to produce something richer and better? We tend to think of censorship as the banning of pernicious rubbish, but censorship is just as much about the suppression of the truth and the substitution of pernicious rubbish instead. If we are silent, we censor the truth.

We are called upon to be salt and light; not salt sealed up in a jar or light hidden under a bushel, but salt in the world's wounds, light shining from our lantern or reflecting, in our looking-glass, the rays of the sun that woke George Herbert. And our desire should be his desire in the poem 'Mattens':

> Teach me thy love to know;
> That this new light, which now I see,
> May both the work and workman show:
> Then by a sunne-beam I will climbe to thee.

For further reading

A bibliography that remained true to the principles of this book would have to include every poet, novelist and dramatist who could possibly claim a place under the umbrella of English literature; for, as I have tried to point out, the purpose of reading is to enrich one's thoughts, sympathies, feelings and knowledge, not as a way of adding another brick or a tasteful ornament to one's personal temple of culture or social acceptability. No writer, therefore, can provide his readers with a list of what they *ought* to read, for there is no ought about it.

Those who have read this book because they are already lovers of literature and are looking for Christian insights and angles will demand one kind of reading list; those who are Christians and who have been persuaded to look, perhaps for the first time, at what literature can offer will demand a rather different sort of reading list.

I was a reader and writer long before I was a Christian, and I think it is true to say that literature was one of the things that led me in the end to Christianity. I would feel dishonest in recommending to newcomers a method which I did not and could not follow myself; and so my advice to them is to forget the books of criticism and analysis to start with and simply devour as many poems, plays and novels as you can. Criticism can be fascinating and helpful, but the text is primary, and it is better to come fresh to a text without any prejudices than to arrive having been told by someone – who may have all sorts of axes to grind – that the work you are about to read is thin and unconvincing, or even great and powerful. Go to the critics after you have met the text and had a chance to respond to it as the writer wishes. It's too late to do anything about Shakespeare, of course: even those who have never read a word know that he is Definitely Great.

Whenever I have quoted a writer in this book, I have been careful to give both the author's name and the title of the work so that, should you have been attracted by a poem or a passage, you can easily find the whole work from which the quotation comes. If the work is in print, you will not need the publisher's name; if it is out of print, the publisher's name will not be much help.

The classics and the works of the English poets have never been easier to get hold of. Oxford Standard Authors, Penguin Classics and Modern Classics, The Everyman Library, Wordsworth Classics and other series will provide, if not the whole body of English literature, at least the skeleton and a lot more. Second-hand bookshops often have hardback editions which are just as cheap but longer lasting and more beautiful. Libraries are not usually very good on poetry, but they will have all the standard anthologies if nothing else. This reading list will, for all these reasons, contain no works of literature but confine itself to further works about literature.

There is a number of books that I have found helpful and informative and which I would not be without. They don't consider literature from any particular spiritual angle, but are fascinating abut what literature is and how it works. E. M. Forster's *Aspects of the Novel* introduces a huge area of study, briefly and entertainingly. It has become something of a classic, having been around since 1927, but is still very readable.

John Press has written a number of books on poetry; they are witty, well-written and draw on a huge variety of poetic styles for their examples. *The Chequer'd Shade* is about difficult poems and obscurity in poetry (old and new) and *The Fire and the Fountain* is about where poetry comes from and how it makes its meanings. Both are published by Oxford. T. S. Eliot is, of course, still an influential critic, and his writings on poetry and drama and the function of the critic can be found in several collections. *On Poetry and Poets* and *The Sacred Wood* are two such. Winifred Nowottny is not an easy read, but for those who want to delve deeply into poetry *The Language Poets Use* is excellent.

Some of the most fascinating ideas, not surprisingly, come from the poets themselves. Eliot has already been mentioned; C. Day Lewis' *The Poetic Image* is clear and straightforward; Robin Skelton has written a number of books on different aspects of the poet's art, of which *Poetic Truth* is my favourite. Robert Graves is opinionated, scholarly and patrician, but he writes with great common sense and he writes beautifully about poetry. He is a pleasure to agree with and fun to argue with. If you can get hold of it, *On Poetry* is a fine collection of talks and essays, and you'll come across a lot more as you search for it. *Winter Pollen* by Ted Hughes is hardly an introductory work, but it is excellent – dense and tightly argued; it deals with lots of different literary topics. *The Redress of Poetry* by Seamus Heaney is calm and loving and fiercely intelligent.

I have not discussed theatre very much in this book; if you want an excellent introduction to theatrical modes and effects you could hardly do better than *The Elements of Drama* by J. L. Styan. He followed this with another fine study entitled *The Dark Comedy*. A book that will be of great interest to Christians is one which explores the ethics and aesthetics of tragedy (which some have said is an impossible form for a Christian writer) and draws the arguments together in terms of the Christian tradition; it is *The Harvest of Tragedy* by T. R. Henn.

If you are looking for an overview of how various critics have filtered literature through their own particular distorting or correcting lenses, there is a very succinct book published by Pelican: George Watson's *The Literary Critics*.

For those those have more time and want something meatier, there is a splendidly comprehensive book which surveys all the different bases for criticism from the Greeks and Romans right up to the middle of this century. It is written in an easy narrative style with masses of quotations, and it does not shirk a final evaluation. It is *Literary Criticism: A Short History* by William K. Wimsatt, Jr. and Cleanth Brooks.

Now for a list of books which consider literature from the point of view of Christian belief and philosophy.

Many of the works in this list are, of course, old friends: those by C. S. Lewis I absorbed as a student, Dorothy Sayers is probably a required text and, at university, I literally sat at the feet of Dame Helen Gardner. Michael Mayne's is a new book, but his ground bass supports many of the themes that have sung in my head for years. Others have been recommended by people whose opinions I have come to trust; but even if that were not so, the very titles suggest that here will be something to set the brain working.

Alter, Robert, and Frank Kermode, eds. *A Literary Guide to the Bible.* Collins, 1987.

Blamires, Harry. *A Short History of English Literature.* Routledge, 1989.

Blanch, Stuart. *The World Our Orphanage.* Epworth, 1972.

Buechner, F. *Telling the Truth: The Gospel as Tragedy, Comedy and Fairy Tale.* Harper & Row, 1977.

Coulson, John. *Religion and Imagination.* OUP, 1981.

Davie, Donald. *God and the Poets.* OUP, 1984.

Detweiler, Robert. *Breaking the Fall: Religious Readings of Contemporary Fiction.* Macmillan, 1989.

Dyson, A. E. *Between Two Worlds: Aspects of Literary Form.* Macmillan, 1972.

Edwards, Michael. *Poetry and Possibility.* Macmillan, 1988.

Edwards, Michael. *Towards a Christian Poetics.* Macmillan, 1984.

Etchells, Ruth. *A Model of Making.* Marshall, Morgan & Scott, 1984.

Etchells, Ruth. *Unafraid to Be.* IVP, 1969.

Frye, Northrop. *The Great Code.* RKP, 1982.

Frye, Roland M. *Shakespeare and Christian Doctrine.* Princeton, 1963.

Gardner, Helen. *Religion and Literature.* Faber, 1971.

Harries, Richard. *Art and the Beauty of God.* Mowbray, 1993.

Harries, Richard. *Questioning Belief.* SPCK, 1995.

Knight, G. Wilson. *The Christian Renaissance.* Macmillan, 1933.

Lewis, C. S. *An Experiment in Criticism.* CUP, 1965.

Lewis, C. S. *Of Other Worlds.* Bles, 1966.

Lewis, C. S. *A Preface to Paradise Lost.* OUP, 1942.

Lewis, C. S. *Selected Literary Essays.* CUP, 1980.

Mayne, Michael. *This Sunrise of Wonder: Letters for the Journey.* Fount, 1995.

Nuttall, A. D. *Overheard by God: Fiction and Prayer in Herbert, Milton, Dante and St John.* Methuen, 1980.

O'Connor, Flannery. *Mystery and Manners.* Edited by S. Fitzgerald and R. Fitzgerald. Faber, 1972.

Phillips, D. Z. *From Fantasy to Faith: The Philosophy of Religion and Twentieth Century Literature.* Macmillan, 1991.

Phillips, D. Z. *Through a Darkening Glass.* Blackwell, 1982.

Rookmaaker, Hans. *Modern Art and the Death of a Culture.* IVP, 1994.

Sayers, Dorothy L. *The Mind of the Maker.* Mowbray, 1994.

Schaeffer, Francis. *Art and the Bible.* Hodder & Stoughton, 1973.

Wheeler, Michael. *Death and the Future Life in Victorian Literature and Theology.* CUP, 1990.